An Episcopal Holy Week Breviary

An Episcopal Holy Week Breviary

Liturgies for use in The Smaller Church

The Reverend Jeffrey A. Mackey, *General Editor*
Formerly Assistant Vice President and
Dean of the College of Arts and Sciences
Nyack College – Nyack, NY & NYC
Currently: Chair, Board of Examining Chaplains, The Diocese of Florida

Unfinished Icons Publishing

Copyrights/Acknowledgements

Scripture quotations, unless otherwise indicated, are from the personal translations of the author.

"Darkness is Gone" by the Iona Community, Copyright [© 1988], Wild Goose Resourced Groups, Iona Community, Scotland – GIA Publications, Inc., exclusive North American Agent, 7404 S. Mason Ave., Chicago, IL 60638 – www.giamusic.com 800.442.1358. All right reserved. Used by permission.

"Laudate Omnes Gentes" by Taize Copyright [© 1978, 1980, 1981], Ateliers et Presses de Taize, Taize Community, France – GIA Publications, Inc., exclusive North American agent, 7404 S. Mason Ave., Chicago, IL 60638 – www.giamusic.com 800.442.1358 All rights reserved. Used by permission.

"Spiritus Jesu Christi" by Taize Copyright [© 1991], Ateliers et Presses de Taize, Taize Community, France – GIA Publications, Inc., exclusive North American agent, 7404 S. Mason Ave., Chicago, IL 60638 – www.giamusic.com 800.442.1358 All rights reserved. Used by permission.

"Bleibet hier" by Taize Copyright [© 1991], Ateliers et Presses de Taize, Taize Community, France – GIA Publications, Inc., exclusive North American agent, 7404 S. Mason Ave., Chicago, IL 60638 – www.giamusic.com 800.442.1358 All rights reserved. Used by permission.

"Jesus, Remember Me" Copyright [© 1981], Ateliers et Presses de Taize, Taize Community, France – GIA Publications, Inc., exclusive North American agent, 7404 S. Mason Ave., Chicago, IL 60638 – www.giamusic.com 800.442.1358 All rights reserved. Used by permission.

"In Remembrance of Thee" [© 1969], Doris Miller. All rights reserved. Used by permission

First edition

Unfinished Icons Publishing
Keystone Heights, Florida

This book is printed on acid-free paper that meets the American National Standards Institute Z39.48 standard. ∞

PRINTED IN THE UNITED STATES OF AMERICA

ISBN-13: 978-1461120414

ISBN-10: 1461120411

Welcome, Invitation, and Helps in Holy Week Worship: A Journey with Jesus Christ

As you worship at an Episcopal Church, **the altar is not the altar of The Episcopal Church, or of our Parish. It is the Table of our Lord Jesus Christ. Therefore, if you are a baptized Christian you are invited to receive the sacrament with your fellow believers.** *You may receive both the bread and wine or just one or the other. You may eat the bread and drink from the chalice, or you may intinct [dip] your bread in the chalice. If you do not wish the sacrament but would like a blessing, come forward and cross your arms across you chest and the priest will pronounce a blessing over you.*

"Rubrics" are those parts of a Breviary, Missal, or Prayer Book which give direction as to how a certain rite is to be enacted. The word "rubric" itself comes from the root of the word "red" and rubrics were, in ancient liturgical books printed in red.

✝✝✝✝✝✝✝

During my tenure as Vicar, then Rector of Trinity Episcopal Church, Melrose, Florida, I watched as people began to make Holy Week a part of their lives. I was so very concerned that the congregation continue these traditions, "in some form." I must acknowledge that Trinity Church people urged me forward. There is one woman and man who spoke so meaningfully of how these services met them and ministered to them during Passion Week 2011.
To Eric and Ann Beshore, the Editor dedicates this volume. May many others find the wonder of Holy Week as did the two of you. God's best to each of you. You are loved.

Table of Contents

An Introduction and an Invitation

This series of services has been compiled and edited specifically for the small church where resources are limited. A small church may have a limited number of lectors, intercessors, Lay Eucharistic Ministers, choir members and other musicians, etc. This is not a bad thing, but a reality which must be taken much into consideration when planning Anglo-Catholic Holy Week liturgies. The compilation makes several other assumptions as well: first, few congregations ever say Compline much less sing it; Taize is unfamiliar to many congregations; few churches have sufficient resources to regularly to enjoy Choral Evensong; and only larger churches can do justice to the historically "cathedral-centered" Easter Vigil."

Right or wrong, these are the assumptions of the editors. Based on these, and on the breadth of the Anglican/Episcopal ethos and the need for coherent salvation-history reading, the services are thus constructed. They have proven themselves deeply encouraging, moving, and edifying to those who have used them. We have purposely incorporated music of various periods and of multiple styles. These, of course, may be so-opted by others chosen by the one presiding.

Over sixty-six years of combined liturgical practice are brought to this Breviary. Two editors are priests in The Episcopal Church and one in the Byzantine Catholic tradition who has spent most of his adult life learning and teaching Anglican liturgy. Many rubics of the Book of Common Prayer allow for vast options at many points in these liturgies and it is highly suggested that those freedoms be exercised to best reflect the local convictions, practices, and preferences. Thanks to Father Guy Linwood Mackey, DTheol, and to Geoffrey Joel Mackey, MA for their editorial assistance.

May God be glorified, our Lord Jesus Christ lifted up, and Holy Spirit given free reign in our hearts during the worship of times of this special week of our liturgical calendar.

Father Jeffrey A. Mackey, Editor
Ash Wednesday, 2012
Vicars Grove at Melrose, Florida

A Service of

Choral Compline

for

Passion Sunday
[Formerly Palm Sunday]

A Hymn

"From Olivet to Calvary"

Ernest F. McGregor, 1879–

Finnish Cavalry March
Thirty Years' War

1. Lift high the tri-umph song to-day! From Ol - i - vet to Cal - va - ry
2. We climb a-gain the wood-ed slopes Of Ol - i - vet and Cal - va - ry;
3. We join the throng to wel-come Him: From Ol - i - vet and Cal - va - ry—
4. We o-pen wide the gates of love! By Ol - i - vet, by Cal - va - ry,

We tread a-gain that an-cient way Our Sav-iour rode in maj - es - ty.
We share with Him those ra-diant hopes, Which led at last to vic - to - ry.
De-scend the heights to shad-ows dim, Thro' death with Him to lib - er - ty.
Ac-claim Him Christ, from God a - bove, Our King, thro' all e - ter - ni - ty.

Let now the loud ho - san - nas ring! The Prince of Peace is pass-ing by;
Let now the loud ho - san - nas ring! The Prince of Peace is pass-ing by;
Let now the loud ho - san - nas ring! The Prince of Peace is pass-ing by;
Let now the loud ho - san - nas ring! The Prince of Peace is pass-ing by;

The Lord of Life, our Sav-iour, King, Goes bravely forth, to reign and die.
The Lord of Life, our Sav-iour, King, Goes glad-ly forth, to live—and die.
The Lord of Life, our Sav-iour, King, Goes humbly forth, to serve—and die.
The Lord of Life, our Sav-iour, King, Goes no-bly forth, no more to die. A-MEN.

Officiant

The Lord Almighty grant us a peace - ful night and a

People

per - fect end. A - men.

Officiant   *People*

Our help is in the name of the Lord; The maker of heaven and earth.

Officiant

Let us confess our sins to God.

Officiant and People [all kneeling]

Almighty God, our heavenly Father:
We have sinned against you,
through our own fault,
in thought, and word, and deed,
and in what we have left undone.
For the sake of your Son our Lord Jesus Christ,
forgive us all our offenses;
and grant that we may serve you
in newness of life,
to the glory of your Name. Amen.

Officiant

May the Almighty God grant us forgiveness of all our
sins, and the grace and comfort of the Holy Spirit. *Amen.*

The Invitatory

Officiant

O God, make speed to save us.

People

O Lord, make haste to help us.

Officiant and People

Glory to the Father, and to the Son, and to the Holy Spi - rit:

as it was in the beginning, is now, and will be for ever. A - men.

The Psalter

Psalm 4 *Cum invocarem*

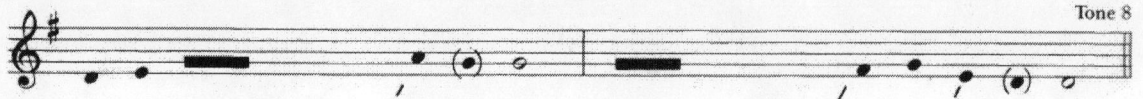

Tone 8

1 *An-swer* me when I call, O God, defender of my cáuse; *
  you set me free when I am hard-pressed;
  have mercy on / me and hear my prayer.

2 "You mortals, how long will you dishonor my glóry? *
  how long will you worship dumb idols
  and run / after fálse gods?"

3 Know that the Lord does wonders for the fáithful; *
  when I call upon the Lord, / he will héar me.

4 Tremble, then, and dó not sin; *
  speak to your heart in si- / lence upón your bed.

5 Offer the appointed sacrifíces, *
  and put your / trust in thé Lord.

6 Many are saying,
  "Oh, that we might see bétter times!" *
  Lift up the light of your countenance up- / on us, Ó Lord.

7 You have put gladness in my héart, *
  more than when grain and / wine and óil increase.

8 I lie down in peace; at once I fáll asleep; *
  for only you, Lord, make me / dwell in sáfety.

The Gloria Patri

At the end of the Psalms, or after each Psalm, is sung

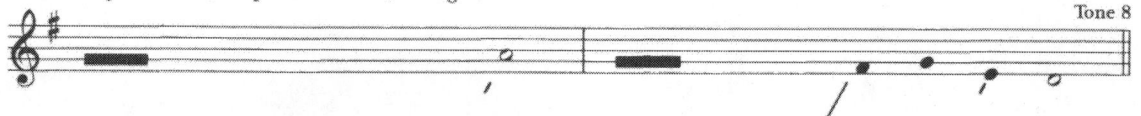

Tone 8

Glory to the Father, and to the Són *
  and to the / Holy Spírit:

As it was in the beginning, is nów *
  and will be for / ever. Ámen.

The Phos Hilaron

1 O gra - cious Light, Lord Je - sus Christ, in you the
2 Now sun - set comes, but light shines forth, the lamps are
3 Wor - thy are you of end - less praise, O Son of

Fa - ther's glo - ry shone. Im - mor - tal, ho - ly,
lit to pierce the night. Praise Fa - ther, Son, and
God, Life - giv - ing Lord; where - fore you are through

blest is he, and blest are you, his ho - ly Son.
Spi - rit: God who dwells in the e - ter - nal light.
all the earth and in the high - est heaven a - dored.

This melody may be sung in rhythmic form: ♪ ♩ ♪ ♩ . Alternative tune: *The Eighth Tune,* 25.

Words: Greek, 3rd cent.; tr. F. Bland Tucker (1895-1984); para. of *O Gracious Light*
Music: *Conditor alme siderum,* plainsong, Mode 4; acc. Bruce Neswick (b. 1956)   LM

The Holy Scripture

Matthew 11:28-30

Come to me, all who labor and are hea-vy-la-den,

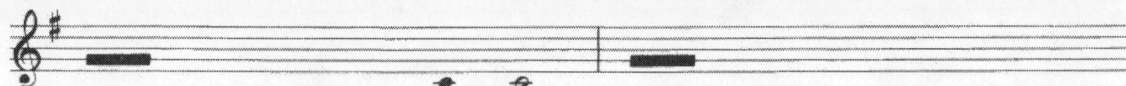

and I will give you rest. Take my yoke upon you, and

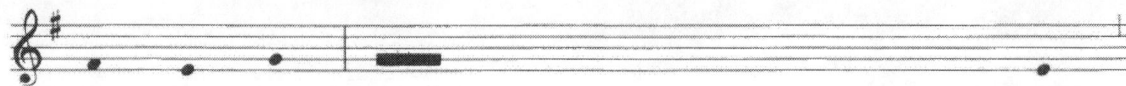

learn from me; For I am gentle and lowly in heart,

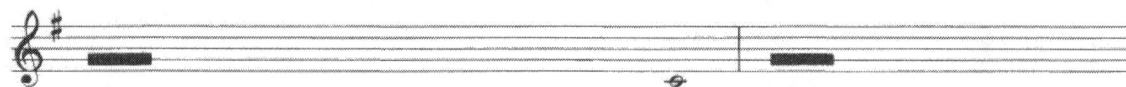

and you will find rest for your souls. For my yoke is easy,

and my burden is light.

People

Thanks be to God.

18

The Homily

The Response

Psalm 134   *Ecce nunc*

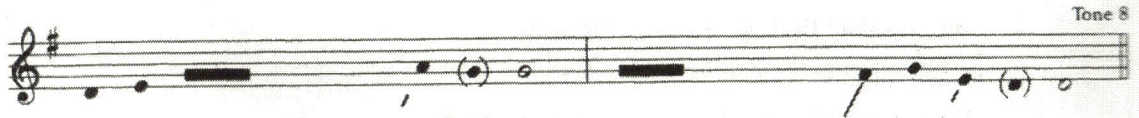

1   *Be-hold* now, bless the Lord, all you servants of the Lórd, *
    you that stand by night in the / house of thé Lord.

2   Lift up your hands in the holy place and bléss the Lord; *
    the Lord who made heaven and earth bless you / out of Zíon.

The Gloria Patri

At the end of the Psalms, or after each Psalm, is sung

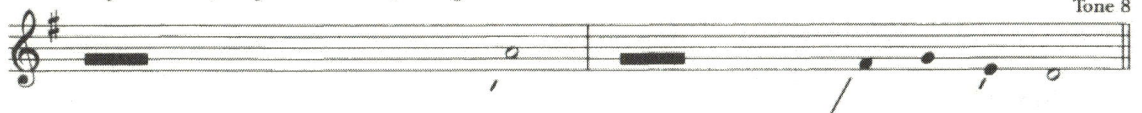

Glory to the Father, and to the Són *
    and to the / Holy Spírit:

As it was in the beginning, is nów *
    and will be for / ever. Ámen.

A Hymn

"O Come and Mourn Awhile"

FREDERICK W. FABER, 1814–1863   JOHN B. DYKES, 1823–1876

1. O   come and mourn with me a - while; O come ye to the Sav-iour's side;
2. Have we no tears to shed for Him, While sol-diers scoff and foes de - ride?
3. Seven times He spake, seven words of love; And all three hours His si - lence cried
4. O   love of God! O sin of man! In this dread act your strength is   tried;

O come, to-geth-er let us mourn: Je - sus, our Lord, is cru - ci - fied!
Ah! look how pa-tient-ly He hangs: Je - sus, our Lord, is cru - ci - fied!
For mer - cy on the souls of   men: Je - sus, our Lord, is cru - ci - fied!
And vic - to - ry re-mains with love: Je - sus, our Lord, is cru - ci - fied! A-MEN.

Then follows

Officiant or Cantor

V. Keep   us,   O   Lord,   as   the   apple   of   your   eye;

People

R. Hide   us   under   the   shadow   of   your   wings.

Officiant   *People*   *Officiant and People*

Lord,   have   mercy.   Christ,   have   mercy.   Lord,   have   mer - cy.

Officiant and People [all kneeling]

Our Father, who art in heaven,
 hallowed be thy Name,
 thy kingdom come,
 thy will be done,
 on earth as it is in heaven.
Give us this day our daily bread.
And forgive us our trespasses,
 as we forgive those
 who trespass against us.
And lead us not into temptation,
 but deliver us from evil.

Lord, hear our prayer. And let our cry come to you.

Let us pray.

Visit this place, O Lord, and drive far from it all snares of the enemy; let your holy angels dwell with us to preserve us in peace; and let your blessing be upon us always; through Jesus Christ our Lord. Amen.

Collect for Palm Sunday

Assist us mercifully with your help, O Lord God of our salvation, that we may enter with joy upon the contemplation of those mighty acts, whereby you have given us life and immortality; through Jesus Christ our Lord. *Amen.*

A Collect for Passion Sunday

Almighty God, whose most dear Son went not up to joy but first he suffered pain, and entered not into glory before he was crucified: Mercifully grant that we, walking in the way of the cross, may find it none other than the way of life and peace; through Jesus Christ our Lord. *Amen.*

A Collect for Sunday

Lord God, whose Son our Savior Jesus Christ triumphed over the powers of death and prepared for us our place in the new Jerusalem: Grant that we, who have this day given thanks for his resurrection, may praise you in that City of which he is the light, and where he lives and reigns for ever and ever. *Amen.*

One of the following collects may be added.

Keep watch, dear Lord, with those who work, or watch, or weep this night, and give your angels charge over those who sleep. Tend the sick, Lord Christ; give rest to the weary, bless the dying, soothe the suffering, pity the afflicted, shield the joyous; and all for your love's sake. Amen.

or this

O God, your unfailing providence sustains the world we live in and the life we live: Watch over those, both night and day, who work while others sleep, and grant that we may never forget that our common life depends upon each other's toil; through Jesus Christ our Lord. Amen.

Silence may be kept, and free intercessions and thanksgivings are invited.

The Song of Simeon

[nunc dimitus]

Unison or harmony

Lord God, you now have set your ser-vant free to go in

peace as prom-ised in your word; my eyes have seen the

Sa-vior, Christ the Lord, pre-pared by you for all the

world to see, to shine on na-tions trapped in dark-est night,

the glo-ry of your peo-ple, and their light.

Words: Rae E. Whitney (b. 1927); para. of *The Song of Simeon*
Music: *Song 1*, melody and bass Orlando Gibbons (1583-1625);
harm. Ralph Vaughan Williams (1872-1958)

♩ =90

10 10. 10 10. 10 10

Officiant *People*

Let us bless the Lord. Thanks be to God.

Officiant

The almighty and mer-ci-ful Lord, Father, Son, and Holy Spi-rit,

People

bless us and keep us. A-men.

A Service

in the

Taize Tradition

For Holy Week

> *"Nothing is more conducive to communion with the living God than meditative common prayer, with its highpoint singing that never ends and that continues in the silence of one's heart when one is alone again. When the mystery of God becomes tangible through the simple beauty of its symbols, when it is not smothered by too many words, then the prayer with others awakens us to heaven's joy on earth."* [The late Brother Roger of Taize]

All songs will be sung in their English text. Please feel free to join in appropriate harmonies as you feel comfortable. Each song is repeated for approximately five minutes as recommended by the Taize Community. Copyright information follows the title page.

"Sing Praises all you People" *"Laudate omnes gentes"*

Laudate omnes gentes, laudate Dominum. Lau-
Sing praises, all you peoples, sing praises to the Lord. Sing

date omnes gentes, laudate Dominum! Lau-
praises, all you peoples, sing praises to the Lord! Sing

Psalm 26 [in unison]

1 Give judgment for me, O LORD,
   for I have lived with integrity; *
   I have trusted in the Lord and have not faltered.

2 Test me, O LORD, and try me; *
   examine my heart and my mind.

3 For your love is before my eyes; *
   I have walked faithfully with you.

4 I have not sat with the worthless, *
  nor do I consort with the deceitful.

5 I have hated the company of evildoers; *
  I will not sit down with the wicked.

6 I will wash my hands in innocence, O LORD, *
  that I may go in procession round your altar,

7 Singing aloud a song of thanksgiving *
  and recounting all your wonderful deeds.

8 LORD, I love the house in which you dwell *
  and the place where your glory abides.

9 As for me, I will live with integrity; *
  redeem me, O LORD, and have pity on me.

10 My foot stands on level ground; *
  in the full assembly I will bless the LORD.

"Spirit of Christ Jesus"   *"Spiritus Jesu Christi"*

Spi - ri - tus Je - su Chri - sti, Spi - ri - tus ca - ri - ta - tis, con -
Spir - it of Christ Je - sus, Spir - it of lov - ing kind - ness, con -

fir - met cor tu - um; con - fir - met cor tu - um.
firm your heart and keep it; con - firm your heart and keep it.

The Holy Scriptures

A Reading from the Epistle to the Hebrews [12:1-3]

Therefore, since we are surrounded by so great a cloud of witnesses, let us also lay aside every weight, and sin which clings so closely, and let us run with endurance the race that is set before us, looking to Jesus, the founder and perfecter of our faith, who for the joy that was set before him endured the cross, despising the shame, and is seated at the right hand of the throne of God. Consider him who endured from sinners such hostility against himself, so that you may not grow weary or fainthearted.

Lector   Here ends the Lesson

Time of Silence [This is an extended time of silence for prayer and meditation. One single light burns as we see the dimming of all light at the impending death of the Son of God].

A Reading from the Gospel of John [13:21-32]

After saying these things, Jesus was troubled in his spirit, and testified, "Truly, truly, I say to you, one of you will betray me." The disciples looked at one another, uncertain of whom he spoke. One of his disciples, whom Jesus loved, was reclining at table close to Jesus, so Simon Peter motioned to him to ask Jesus of whom he was speaking. So that disciple, leaning back against Jesus, said to him, "Lord, who is it?" Jesus answered, "It is he to whom I will give this morsel of bread when I have dipped it." So when he had dipped the morsel, he gave it to Judas, the son of Simon Iscariot. Then after he had taken the morsel, Satan entered into him. Jesus said to him, "What you are going to do, do quickly." Now no one at the table knew why he said this to him. Some thought that, because Judas had the moneybag, Jesus was telling him, "Buy what we need for the feast," or that he should give something to the poor. So, after receiving the morsel of bread, he immediately went out. And it was night.

Lector   Here ends the Lesson

The Intercessions The *Congregation* responds, *"Lord hear our prayer"*

Intercessor   God, the creator and savior, source of peace for the entire world, be our peace, our life, today. Response

Intercessor   Christ, you call us to yourself through your outstretched arms on the cross – draw the whole world to you. Response

Intercessor   Lord Christ, help us remember the needs of others around us and use us as instruments of your love and care. Response

Intercessor   Lord, in seeking the lost sheep, keep us ever aware that we are witnesses to the work you do, by grace, in the human heart, and may we draw others to you. Response.

Intercessor   O Holy Spirit, the comfort of all who love you awaken us to a love that forgives. Help us receive forgiveness and to forgive others as has forgiven us. Response.

"Stay with Me" *"Bleibet hier"*

Stay with me, remain here with me, watch and pray,
watch and pray.

Blei - bet hier und wa - chet mit mir, wa - chet und
be - tet, wa - chet und be - tet.

The Lord's Prayer

Our Father, who art in heaven,
 hallowed be thy Name,
 thy kingdom come, thy will be done,
 on earth as it is in heaven.
Give us this day our daily bread.
And forgive us our trespasses, as we forgive those
 who trespass against us.
And lead us not into temptation,
 but deliver us from evil.
For thine is the kingdom and the power
 and the glory, forever and ever. Amen.

The Closing Prayer

   Lord Christ, enable us to watch with you through the
nights of sin's darkness for the sake of ourselves and
others. Remind us of the incessant working of Holy
Spirit in us an in all peoples. By your grace help us with
our accepting of your forgiveness and may we love you
more and more, through Christ our Lord. *Amen.*

[Please turn the page for *"Jesus, Remember Me"*]

"Jesus, Remember Me"

Celebrant   Go in peace.
People   *In the Name of Christ. Amen.*

Pray and Meditate as long as you wish. The service is ended.

Choral Evensong

in

Holy Week

The Processional Hymn *"Day is Dying in the West"*

Mary A. Lathbury, 1841-1913

William F. Sherwin, 1826-1888

1. Day is dy - ing in the west, Heaven is touch-ing earth with rest;
2. Lord of life, be - neath the dome Of the u - ni - verse, Thy home,
3. While the deep-ening shad-ows fall, Heart of love, en - fold - ing all,
4. When for - ev - er from our sight Pass the stars, the day, the night,

Wait and wor - ship while the night Sets her eve - ning lamps a - light
Gath - er us, who seek Thy face, To the fold of Thy em-brace,
Through the glo - ry and the grace Of the stars that veil Thy face,
Lord of an - gels, on our eyes Let e - ter - nal morn - ing rise

REFRAIN

Through all the sky.
For Thou art nigh. Ho - ly, ho - ly, ho - ly, Lord God of hosts! Heaven and
Our hearts as - cend.
And shad-ows end.

earth are full of Thee; Heaven and earth are prais-ing Thee, O Lord most high!

35

The Psalter – Psalm [50: 1-24]   *Deus deorum*

1 The Lord, the God of gods, has <u>spoken</u>; *
 he has called the earth from the rising of the sun to
  its <u>setting</u>.

2 Out of Zion, perfect in its <u>beauty</u>, *
 God reveals himself in <u>glory</u>.

3 Our God will come and will not keep <u>silence</u>; *
 before him there is a consuming flame,
 and round about him a raging <u>storm</u>.

4 He calls the heavens and the earth from <u>above</u> *
 to witness the judgment of his <u>people</u>.

5 "Gather before me my loyal <u>followers</u>, *
 those who have made a covenant with me
 and sealed it with <u>sacrifice</u>."

6 Let the heavens declare the rightness of his <u>cause</u>; *
 for God himself is <u>judge</u>.

7 Hear, O my people, and I will speak:
 "O Israel, I will bear witness against <u>you</u>; *
 for I am God, your <u>God</u>.

8 I do not accuse you because of your <u>sacrifices</u>; *
    your offerings are always be<u>fore me</u>.

9 I will take no bull-calf from your <u>stalls</u>, *
    nor he-goats out of your <u>pens</u>;

10 For all the beasts of the forest are <u>mine</u>, *
    the herds in their thousands upon the <u>hills</u>.

11 I know every bird in the <u>sky</u>, *
    and the creatures of the fields are in my <u>sight</u>.

12 If I were hungry, I would not tell <u>you</u>, *
    for the whole world is mine and all that is <u>in it</u>.

13 Do you think I eat the flesh of <u>bulls</u>, *
    or drink the blood of <u>goats</u>?

14 Offer to God a sacrifice of <u>thanksgiving</u> *
    and make good your vows to the Most <u>High</u>.

15 Call upon me in the day of <u>trouble</u>; *
    I will deliver you, and you shall honor <u>me</u>."

16 But to the wicked God <u>says</u>: *
    "Why do you recite my statutes,
    and take my covenant upon your <u>lips</u>;

17 Since you refuse <u>discipline</u>, *
    and toss my words behind your <u>back</u>?

18 When you see a thief, you make him your <u>friend</u>, *
    and you cast in your lot with <u>adulterers</u>.

19 You have loosed your lips for <u>evil</u>, *
and harnessed your tongue to a <u>lie</u>.

20 You are always speaking evil of your <u>brother</u> *
and slandering your own mother's <u>son</u>.

21 These things you have done, and I kept <u>still</u>, *
and you thought that I am like <u>you</u>."

22 I have made my accu<u>sation</u>; *
I have put my case in order before your <u>eyes</u>.

23 Consider this well, you who forget <u>God</u>, *
lest I rend you and there be none to de<u>liver you</u>.

24 Whoever offers me the sacrifice of thanksgiving
honors <u>me</u>; *
but to those who keep in my way will I show
the salvation of <u>God</u>."

Glory be to the Father, and to the <u>Son</u> and to the Holy
<u>Ghost;</u>
As it was in the beginning is <u>now</u>
and will be forever. A<u>men</u>.

The First Reading – Hebrews [4:1-10]

Therefore, since the promise of entering his rest still stands, let us be careful that none of you be found to have fallen short of it. For we also have had the good news proclaimed to us, just as they did; but the message they heard was of no value to them, because they did not share the faith of those who obeyed. Now we who have believed enter that rest, just as God has said,

"So I declared on oath in my anger,
'They shall never enter my rest.'"

And yet his works have been finished since the creation of the world. For somewhere he has spoken about the seventh day in these words: "On the seventh day God rested from all his works." And again in the passage above he says, "They shall never enter my rest."

Therefore since it still remains for some to enter that rest, and since those who formerly had the good news proclaimed to them did not go in because of their disobedience, God again set a certain day, calling it "Today." This he did when a long time later he spoke through David, as in the passage already quoted:

"Today, if you hear his voice,
do not harden your hearts."

For if Joshua had given them rest, God would not have spoken later about another day. There remains, then, a Sabbath-rest for the people of God; for anyone who enters God's rest also rests from their works, just as God did from his.

Lector   Here ends the Lesson

[please turn the page for the Magnificat]

The Song of Mary *(The Magnificat)* Luke [1:45-56]

Timothy Dudley-Smith

Walter Greatorex (1877-1949)
Woodlands 10 10 10 10

1. Tell out, my soul, the great-ness of the Lord! Un-num-ber'd bles-sings, give my spi-rit voice; Ten-der to me the pro-mise of His word; In God my Sa-vior shall my heart re-joice.
2. Tell out, my soul, the great-ness of His Name! Make known His might, the deeds His arm has done; His mer-cy sure, from age to age the same; His Ho-ly Name— the Lord, the Might-y One.
3. Tell out, my soul, the great-ness of His might! Pow'rs and do-mi-nions lay their glo-ry by. Proud hearts and stub-born wills are put to flight, The hun-gry fed, the hum-ble lift-ed high.
4. Tell out, my soul, the glo-ries of His word! Firm is His pro-mise, and His mer-cy sure. Tell out, my soul, the great-ness of the Lord To chil-dren's chil-dren and for e-ver-more!

The Second Reading – Romans [8: 1–11]

There is therefore now no condemnation for those who are in Christ Jesus. For the law of the Spirit of life has set you free in Christ Jesus from the law of sin and death. For God has done what the law, weakened by the flesh, could not do. By sending his own Son in the likeness of sinful flesh and for sin, he condemned sin in the flesh, 4 in order that the righteous requirement of the law might be fulfilled in us, who walk not according to the flesh but according to the Spirit. For those who live according to the flesh set their minds on the things of the flesh, but those who live according to the Spirit set their minds on the things of the Spirit. For to set the mind on the flesh is death, but to set the mind on the Spirit is life and peace. For the mind that is set on the flesh is hostile to God, for it does not submit to God's law; indeed, it cannot. Those who are in the flesh cannot please God.

You, however, are not in the flesh but in the Spirit, if in fact the Spirit of God dwells in you. Anyone who does not have the Spirit of Christ does not belong to him. But if Christ is in you, although the body is dead because of sin, the Spirit is life because of righteousness. If the Spirit of him who raised Jesus from the dead dwells in you, he who raised Christ Jesus from the dead will also give life to your mortal bodies through his Spirit who dwells in you. So then, brothers, we are debtors, not to the flesh, to live according to the flesh.

[Please turn the page for the Nunc dimittis]

The Song of Simeon (*Nunc dimittis*) Luke [2:29-32]

Unison or harmony

Lord God, you now have set your ser-vant free to go in
peace as prom-ised in your word; my eyes have seen the
Sa-vior, Christ the Lord, pre-pared by you for all the
world to see, to shine on na-tions trapped in dark-est night,
the glo-ry of your peo-ple, and their light.

Words: Rae E. Whitney (b. 1927); para. of *The Song of Simeon*
Music: *Song 1*, melody and bass Orlando Gibbons (1583-1625);
harm. Ralph Vaughan Williams (1872-1958)

♩=90
10 10. 10 10. 10 10

The Apostles' Creed

Officiant and People together, all standing

I believe in God, the Father almighty,
    maker of heaven and earth;
And in Jesus Christ his only Son our Lord;
    who was conceived by the Holy Ghost,
    born of the Virgin Mary,
    suffered under Pontius Pilate,
    was crucified, dead, and buried.
    He descended into hell.
    The third day he rose again from the dead.
    He ascended into heaven,
    and sitteth on the right hand of God the Father
    Almighty.
    From thence he shall come to judge the quick and the
    dead.
I believe in the Holy Ghost,
    the holy catholic Church,
    the communion of saints,
    the forgiveness of sins,
    the resurrection of the body,
    and the life everlasting. Amen.

The Prayers

The people kneel or sit as needed.

Officiant   The Lord be with you.
People   And with thy spirit.
Officiant   Let us pray.

Officiant and People

Our Father, who art in heaven,
    hallowed be thy Name,
    thy kingdom come,
    thy will be done,
        on earth as it is in heaven.
Give us this day our daily bread.
And forgive us our trespasses,
    as we forgive those who trespass against us.
And lead us not into temptation,
    but deliver us from evil.
For thine is the kingdom, and the power, and the glory,
    for ever and ever. Amen.

That this evening may be holy, good, and peaceful,
We entreat thee, O Lord.

That thy holy angels may lead us in paths of peace and
goodwill,
We entreat thee, O Lord.

That we may be pardoned and forgiven for our sins
and offenses,
We entreat thee, O Lord.

That there may be peace to thy Church and to the whole
world,
We entreat thee, O Lord.

That we may depart this life in thy faith and fear, and
not be condemned before the great judgment seat
of Christ,
We entreat thee, O Lord.

That we may be bound together by thy Holy Spirit in the communion of the Blessed Virgin Mary, St. Joseph, St. Dominic, and all thy saints, entrusting one another and all our life to Christ,
We entreat thee, O Lord.

The Collect of the Day

O God, by the passion of your blessed Son you made an instrument of shameful death to be for us the means of life: Grant us so to glory in the cross of Christ, that we may gladly suffer shame and loss for the sake of your Son our Savior Jesus Christ; who lives and reigns with you and the Holy Spirit, one God, for ever and ever. *Amen.*

A Collect for Protection

O God, who art the life of all who live, the light of the faithful, the strength of those who labor, and the repose of the dead: We thank thee for the timely blessings of the day, and humbly beseech thy merciful protection all the night. Bring us, we pray thee, in safety to the morning hours; through him who died for us and rose again, thy Son our Savior Jesus Christ. *Amen.*

O God, who dost manifest in thy servants the signs of thy presence: Send forth upon us the Spirit of love, that in companionship with one another thine abounding grace may increase among us; through Jesus Christ our Lord. *Amen.*

Intercessions and thanksgivings are invited

A Prayer of St. Chrysostom

Almighty God, who hast given us grace at this time with one accord to make our common supplication unto thee; and hast promised through thy well-beloved Son that when two or three are gathered together in his Name thou wilt be in the midst of them: Fulfill now, O Lord, the desires and petitions of thy servants as may be best for us; granting us in this world knowledge of thy truth, and in the world to come life everlasting. *Amen.*

Then is said

Officiant Let us bless the Lord.
People *Thanks be to God.*

A Service

Of Divine Healing

Wednesday Noon of

Holy Week

The Liturgy of the Word

The Entrance Hymn

"There Is a Healing Branch That Flows"

RETREAT L.M.

Albert B. Simpson, 1843-1919

Melody by Thomas Hastings, 1784-1872

1. There	is	a	heal-ing	branch that	grows	Where	ev-	ery
2. There	is	an	old	ap-point-ed	way	For	those	who
3. There	is	an	ord'-nance that	has	stood	Since	Is-	rael
4. There	is	a	great Phy-si-cian	still	Whose	hand	has	

bit-ter	Ma-rah	flows;	This	is	our	health-re-		
heark-en	and	o-bey;	A-bove	the	gate	these		
crossed	the	part-ed	flood;	It	stands	to-day	for	
all	its	an-cient	skill;	At	His	com-mand	our	

new-ing	tree.	"I	am	the	Lord	that	heal-eth thee."
words	we	see:	"I	am	the	Lord	that heal-eth thee."
you	and	me—	"I	am	the	Lord	that heal-eth thee."
pains	will	flee—	"I	am	the	Lord	that heal-eth thee."

The Opening Acclamation

Celebrant Bless the Lord who forgives all our sins.
People   His mercy endures forever.

49

Celebrant   Almighty God, to you all hearts are open, all desire know, and from you no secrets are hid: Cleanse the thoughts of our hearts by the inspiration of your Holy Spirit, that we may perfectly love you, and worthily magnify your holy Name, through Christ our Lord. *Amen.*

Celebrant Lord have mercy.
People   Christ have mercy.
Celebrant Lord have mercy. The Lord be with you.
People   And also with you.
Celebrant Let us pray.

O God of Peace, you have taught us that in returning and rest we shall be saved; in quietness and confidence shall be our strength; by the might of your Sprit, lift us, we pray, to your presence, where we may be still and know that you are God; through Jesus Christ our Lord, who with you and Holy Spirit lives and reigns, one God, for ever and ever. *Amen.*

The Lessons Appointed [These lections are from the "B" year of the Revised Common Lectionary]

A Reading from the Prophet Isaiah [50:4-9a]

4 The Lord GOD has given me
   the tongue of those who are taught,
that I may know how to sustain with a word
   him who is weary.
Morning by morning he awakens;
   he awakens my ear
   to hear as those who are taught.

5 The Lord GOD has opened my ear,
    and I was not rebellious;
    I turned not backwards.
6 I gave my back to those who strike,
    and my cheeks to those who pull out the beard;
I hid not my face
    from disgrace and spitting.
7 But the Lord GOD helps me;
    therefore I have not been disgraced;
therefore I have set my face like a flint,
    and I know that I shall not be put to shame.
 8 He who vindicates me is near.
Who will contend with me?
    Let us stand up together.
Who is my adversary?
    Let him come near to me.
9 Behold, the Lord GOD helps me;
    who will declare me guilty?

The Psalm [70:1-6]   *Deus, in adjutorium*

1 Be pleased, O God, to deliver me; *
    O LORD, make haste to help me.

2 Let those who seek my life be ashamed
    and altogether dismayed; *
    let those who take pleasure in my misfortune
    draw back and be disgraced.

3 Let those who say to me "Aha!" and gloat over me turn
back, *
    because they are ashamed.

4 Let all who seek you rejoice and be glad in you; *
    let those who love your salvation say for ever,
    "Great is the LORD!"

5 But as for me, I am poor and needy; *
   come to me speedily, O God.

6 You are my helper and my deliverer; *
   O LORD, do not tarry.

A Sequence Hymn

"Ask ye what Great Thing I Know?"

JOHANN C. SCHWEDLER, 1672-1730
Tr. by BENJAMIN H. KENNEDY, 1804-1889   H. A. CÉSAR MALAN, 1787-1864

1. Ask ye what great thing I know
2. Who de - feats my fier - cest foes?
3. Who is life in life to me?
4. This is that great thing I know;

That de - lights and stirs me so? What the high re -
Who con - soles my sad - dest woes? Who re - vives my
Who the death of death will be? Who will place me
This de - lights and stirs me so: Faith in Him who

ward I win? Whose the name I glo - ry in?
faint - ing heart, Heal - ing all its hid - den smart?
on His right, With the count - less hosts of light?
died to save, Him who tri - umphed o'er the grave,

Je - sus Christ, the Cru - ci - fied.
Je - sus Christ, the Cru - ci - fied.
Je - sus Christ, the Cru - ci - fied.
Je - sus Christ, the Cru - ci - fied.   A - MEN.

The Holy Gospel of our Lord Jesus Christ According to John [13:21-32]

After saying these things, Jesus was troubled in his spirit, and testified, "Truly, truly, I say to you, one of you will betray me." The disciples looked at one another, uncertain of whom he spoke. One of his disciples, whom Jesus loved, was reclining at table close to Jesus, so Simon Peter motioned to him to ask Jesus of whom he was speaking. So that disciple, leaning back against Jesus, said to him, "Lord, who is it?" Jesus answered, "It is he to whom I will give this morsel of bread when I have dipped it." So when he had dipped the morsel, he gave it to Judas, the son of Simon Iscariot. 27Then after he had taken the morsel, Satan entered into him. Jesus said to him, "What you are going to do, do quickly." Now no one at the table knew why he said this to him. Some thought that, because Judas had the money bag, Jesus was telling him, "Buy what we need for the feast", or that he should give something to the poor. So, after receiving the morsel of bread, he immediately went out. And it was night.

When he had gone out, Jesus said, "Now is the Son of Man glorified, and God is glorified in him. If God is glorified in him, God will also glorify him in himself, and glorify him at once.

Celebrant [or Deacon] The Holy Gospel of our Lord Jesus Christ According to John.
People Glory to you, Lord Christ

After the Gospel is read

Celebrant The Gospel of the Lord
People Praise to you, Lord Christ.

The Homily

The Litany of Healing *[Intercessor chooses either "A" or "B" – people are invited to audibly declare the first names of those for whom they seek prayer]*

Celebrant Let us name before God, those for whom we offer our prayers.

Intercessor [Litany A]

God the Father, your will for all people is health and salvation;
We praise you and thank you, O God.

God the Son, you came that we might have life, and might have it more abundantly;
We praise you and thank you, O God.

God, Holy Spirit, you make our bodies the temple of your presence;
We praise you and thank you, O God.

Holy Trinity, one God, in you we live and move and have our being;
We praise you and thank you, O God.

Lord, grant your healing grace to all who are sick, injured, or disabled, that they may be whole;
Hear us, O Lord of life.

Grant to all who seek your guidance, and to all who are lonely, anxious, or despondent, a knowledge of your will and an awareness of your presence;
Hear us, O Lord of life.

54

Mend broken relationships, and restore those in emotional distress to soundness of mind and serenity of spirit;
Hear us, O Lord of life.

Bless physicians, nurses, and all others who minister to the suffering, granting them wisdom and skill, sympathy and patience.
Hear us, O Lord of life.

Grant to the dying peace, and a holy death, and uphold by thy grace and consolation of Holy Spirit those who are bereaved;
Hear us, O Lord of life.

Restore to wholeness whatever is broken by human sin, in our lives, our nation, in the world;
Hear us, O Lord of life.

You are the Lord who does wonders;
You have declared your power among the people;

With you, O Lord, is the well of life;
And in your life we see the light;

Hear us, O Lord of life;
Heal us and make us whole.

Let us pray.

Or this

Intercessor [Litany B]

God of grace, you nurture us with a love deeper than we
know, and your will for us is health and salvation;
We praise you, and thank you, O God.

God of love, you enter into our lives, our pain and our
brokenness, and you stretch out your healing hands to
us wherever we are;
We praise you, and thank you, O God.

God of strength, you fill us with your presences and send
us forth in love and healing among those we meet;
We praise you, and thank you, O God.

Touch and heal our bodies suffering from sickness,
injury or disability, and make us whole again;
Hear us, O God of life.

Touch and heal our minds from darkness, confusion, and
doubt, and fill them with your light;
Hear us, O God of life.

Touch and heal our hearts burdened by anguish,
despair, and isolation, and set us free in love;
Hear us, O God of life.

Break the bonds of imprisonment t fear, compulsion, and
addiction;
Come with your healing power, O Lord;

Fill us with peace in our grief from separation and loss;
Come with your healing power, O Lord;

Take our hands in dying, and bring us through death
into your loving presence;
Come with your healing power, O Lord;

Work through all who share in your ministry of healing,
and renew us in compassion and strength;
Come with your healing power, O Lord;

Restore to wholeness all that has been broken by our
sins;
Come with your healing power, O Lord.

Rejoicing in the communion of the Blessed Virgin Mary,
St. Joseph, [_____], and all your Saints, we
entrust ourselves and one another,
And all our life to Christ our God.

A period of silence follows

*The Celebrant concludes the litany with one of the
following or some other suitable Collect:*

Almighty God, giver of life and health; send your blessing
on all who are sick, and upon those who minister to
them, that all weakness may be vanquished by the
triumph of the risen Christ; who lives and reigns for ever
and ever. *Amen.*

Or this:

Heavenly Father, you have promised to hear what we ask
in the Name of your Son: accept and fulfill our petitions,
we pray, not as we ask in our ignorance, nor as we
deserve in our sinfulness, but as you know and love us in
your Son Jesus Christ our Lord. *Amen.*

Or this:

O Lord our God, accept the fervent prayers of your people; in the multitude of your mercies look with compassion upon us and all who turn to you for help; for you are gracious , O lover of souls, and to you we give glory, Father, Son and Holy Spirit, now and forever.
Amen

The Confession of Sin

Celebrant or Deacon   Let us confess our sins unto Almighty God.

All   Most merciful God, we confess that we have sinned against you in thought, word, and deed, by what we have done, and by what we have left undone. We have not loved you with our whole heart; we have not loved our neighbors as ourselves. We are truly sorry and we humbly repent. For the sake of your Son Jesus Christ, have mercy on us and forgive us; that we may delight in your will and walk in your ways, to the glory of your Name. *Amen.*

Celebrant   Almighty God have mercy on you, forgive you all your sins through our Lord Jesus Christ, strengthen you in all goodness, and by the power of the Holy Spirit keep you in eternal life. *Amen.*

The Celebrant now invites those who wish the laying on of hands and anointing with oil to approach the altar rail.

Celebrant   Savior of the world, by your cross and precious blood you have redeemed us.

People   Save us and help us we humbly beseech you, O Lord.

Celebrant   The Almighty Lord, who is a strong tower to all who put their trust in him, to whom all things in heaven, on earth, and under the earth bow and obey: Be now and evermore your defense, and make you know and feel that the only Name under heaven, given for health and salvation is the Name of our Lord Jesus Christ. *Amen.*

After you have been anointed and prayer has been made, please return to your seat.

Celebrant   As you are outwardly anointed with this holy oil, so may our heavenly Father grant you the inward anointing of the Holy Spirit. Of his great mercy, may he forgive you your sins; release you from suffering, and restore you to wholeness and strength. May he deliver you from all evil, preserve you in all goodness, and bring you to everlasting life; through Jesus Christ our Lord. *Amen.*

The Peace

Celebrant The peace of the Lord be always with you.
People   And also with you.

The Holy Eucharist

The Offertory [An appropriate Hymn or chorus of healing may be sung]

The Doxology *all stand*

> Praise God from whom all blessings flow;
> Praise him all creatures here, below.
> Praise him above, ye heavenly hosts.
> Praise Father, Son, and Holy Ghost. Amen.

The people remain standing.

The Sursum Corda

Celebrant The Lord be with you.
People   And also with you.
Celebrant Lift up your hearts.
People   We lift them to the Lord.
Celebrant Let us give thanks to the Lord our God.
People   It is right to give him thanks and praise.

Celebrant It is right, and a good and joyful thing, always and everywhere to give thanks to you, Father Almighty, Creator of heaven and earth through Jesus Christ our Lord. For our sins he was lifted high upon the cross, that he might draw the whole world to himself; and, by his suffering and death, he became the source of eternal salvation for all who put their trust in him.

Therefore we praise you, joining our voices with Angels and Archangels and with all the company of heaven, who

for ever sing this hymn to proclaim the glory of your
Name:

Celebrant and People

Holy, holy, holy Lord, God of power and might,
heaven and earth are full of your glory.
  Hosanna in the highest.
Blessed is he who comes in the name of the Lord.
  Hosanna in the highest.

The people stand or kneel.

Celebrant

We give thanks to you, O God, for the goodness and love
which you have made known to us in creation; in the
calling of Israel to be your people; in your Word spoken
through the prophets; and above all in the Word made
flesh, Jesus, your Son. For in these last days you sent
him to be incarnate from the Virgin Mary, to be the
Savior and Redeemer of the world. In him, you have
delivered us from evil, and made us worthy to stand
before you. In him, you have brought us out of error
into truth, out of sin into righteousness, out of death into
life.

On the night before he died for us, our Lord Jesus Christ
took bread; and when he had given thanks to you, he
broke it, and gave it to his disciples, and said, "Take, eat:
This is my Body, which is given for you. Do this for the
remembrance of me."

After supper he took the cup of wine; and when he had
given thanks, he gave it to them, and said, "Drink this,
all of you: This is my Blood of the new Covenant, which is

shed for you and for many for the forgiveness of sins. Whenever you drink it, do this for the remembrance of me."

Therefore, according to his command, O Father,

Celebrant and People

We remember his death,
We proclaim his resurrection,
We await his coming in glory;

Celebrant And we offer our sacrifice of praise and thanksgiving to you, O Lord of all; presenting to you, from your creation, this bread and this wine.

We pray you, gracious God, to send your Holy Spirit upon these gifts that they may be the Sacrament of the Body of Christ and his Blood of the new Covenant. Unite us to your Son in his sacrifice, that we may be acceptable through him, being sanctified by the Holy Spirit. In the fullness of time, put all things in subjection under your Christ, and bring us to that heavenly country where, with the Blessed Virgin Mary, St. Joseph, [_____. and] all your Saints, we may enter the everlasting heritage of your sons and daughters; through Jesus Christ our Lord, the firstborn of all creation, the head of the Church, and the author of our salvation.

By him, and with him, and in him, in the unity of the Holy Spirit all honor and glory is yours, Almighty Father, now and for ever. *AMEN.*

The Lord's Prayer

Celebrant And now as our Savior Christ has taught us, we are bold to say,
Celebrant and People Our Father, who art in heaven,
 hallowed be thy Name,
 thy kingdom come, thy will be done,
 on earth as it is in heaven.
Give us this day our daily bread.
And forgive us our trespasses,
 as we forgive those
 who trespass against us.
And lead us not into temptation,
 but deliver us from evil.
For thine is the kingdom and the power
 and the glory, forever and ever. *Amen.*

The Holy Communion

Celebrant Christ our Passover is sacrificed for us.
People   Therefore let us keep the feast.

Celebrant Lamb of God, you take away the sins of the world. *People* Have mercy on us.
Celebrant Lamb of God, you take away the sins of the world. *People* Have mercy upon us.
Celebrant Lamb of God, you take away the sins of the world. *People* Grant us peace.
Celebrant The gifts of God for the people of God. Take them in remembrance that Christ died for you, and feed on him in your hearts by faith.

The Postcommunion Prayer & Priestly Blessing

Celebrant Let us pray.
Celebrant and People Almighty and eternal God, so draw our hearts to you; so guide our minds; so fill our imaginations; so control our wills; that we may be wholly

yours, utterly dedicated to you, and then use us, we pray, as your will, and always too your glory and the welfare of your people; through our Lord and Savior Jesus Christ. *Amen.*

Celebrant May God the Father bless you; God the Son heal you; God the Holy Spirit give you strength. May God, the Holy and undivided Trinity guard your body, save your soul, and bring you safely to his heavenly country; where he lives and reigns for ever and ever. *Amen.*

The Processional Hymn

"Jesus, Breathe Thy Spirit on Me"

HOLY MANNA 8.7.8.7.D.
Albert B. Simpson, 1843-1919 / William Moore, 19th century

1. Je - sus, breathe Thy Spir-it on me, Teach me how to breathe Thee in,
2. Breath-ing out my sin-ful na-ture, Thou hast borne it all for me;
3. I am breath-ing out my long-ings, In Thy list-'ning lov-ing ear,

Help me pour in-to Thy bos-om All my life of self and sin.
Breath-ing in Thy cleans-ing full-ness, Find-ing all my life in Thee.
I am breath-ing in Thy an-swers, Still-ing ev-ery doubt and fear.

I am breath-ing out my own life, That I may be filled with Thine;
I am breath-ing out my sor-row, On Thy kind and gen-tle breast;
I am breath-ing ev-ery mo-ment, Draw-ing all my life from Thee;

Let - ting go my strength and weak-ness, Breath-ing   in Thy life di- vine.
Breath-ing   in Thy joy and com - fort, Breath-ing   in Thy peace and rest.
Breath by breath I   live up - on   Thee, Bless - ed   Spir - it, breathe in me.

The Dismissal

People respond: Thanks be to God.

A Service

of

Tenebrae

The one (or ones) planning this liturgy, may wish to find other sources of music either of the more ancient or of the more contemporary. Particularly where the "Worthy is the Lamb" is sung, it would be most appropriate to find the contemporary piece "Worthy is the Lamb," by Don Wyrtzen. Remember to be faithful to copyright laws. Other appropriate readings may be substituted by the liturgical planner(s). At the ++ a loud noise is made to represent the resurrection just prior to the Christ candle being returned to its place.

The Bidding

Officiant: Tenebrae is a "Service of Darkness." All the purpose of our time before the altar is to rehearse again God's love for the creation and the creature, love that took our Savior, Jesus to Calvary's cross and into death itself. Our worship space will darken as evening falls and each candle is extinguished. will grow gradually darker as each candle is extinguished. Christ, the world's true light will go metaphorically to the grave and then reappear in resurrection glow! It is requested that we each leave the church in silence and return home meditating on what we have heard and seen. [You may even want to consider traveling all the way home in silent contemplation.]

Officiant   The Lord be with you.
People   And also with you.
Officiant   Let us pray.

Lord God, whose blessed Son our Savior gave his body to be whipped and his face to be spit upon: Give us grace to accept joyfully the sufferings of the present time, confident of the glory that shall be revealed; through Jesus Christ your Son our Lord, who lives and reigns with you and the Holy Spirit, one God, for ever and ever. Amen.

A Reading from the Lamentations [1:1-5]

[1]How lonely sits the city
  that was full of people!
  How like a widow has she become,
  she who was great among the nations!
  She who was a princess among the provinces
  has become a slave.

2 She weeps bitterly in the night,
  with tears on her cheeks;
  among all her lovers
  she has none to comfort her;
  all her friends have dealt treacherously with her;
  they have become her enemies.

3 Judah has gone into exile because of affliction
  and hard servitude;
  she dwells now among the nations,
  but finds no resting place;
  her pursuers have all overtaken her
  in the midst of her distress.

4 The roads to Zion mourn,
  for none come to the festival;
  all her gates are desolate;
  her priests groan;
  her virgins have been afflicted,
  and she herself suffers bitterly.

5 Her foes have become the head;
  her enemies prosper,
  because the LORD has afflicted her
  for the multitude of her transgressions;
  her children have gone away,
  captives before the foe. [1]

Officiant   Deliver me, O Lord, from the hands of the wicked.

People   *From the clutches of the evildoers and the oppressor.*

Officiant   On the Mount of Olives, Jesus prayed to the Father.

People   *Father, if it be possible let this cup pass from me. The spirit is indeed willing, but the flesh is weak.*

Officiant   Watch and pray that you may not enter into temptation

People   *The spirit indeed is willing, but the flesh is weak.*

A Responsive Reading from the Prophet Isaiah
[53:4-12]

Officiant He grew up before him like a tender shoot, and like a root out of dry ground. He had no beauty or majesty to attract us to him, nothing in his appearance that we should desire him.

People *He was despised and rejected by men, a man of sorrows, and familiar with suffering. Like one from whom men hide their faces he was despised, and we esteemed him not.*

Officiant Surely he took up our infirmities and carried our sorrows, yet we considered him stricken by God, smitten by him, and afflicted.

People *But he was pierced for our transgressions, he was crushed for our iniquities; the punishment that brought us peace was upon him, and by his wounds we are healed.*

Officiant We all, like sheep, have gone astray, each of us has turned to his own way; and the LORD has laid on him the iniquity of us all.

People *He was oppressed and afflicted, yet he did not open his mouth; he was led like a lamb to the slaughter, and as a sheep before her shearers is silent, so he did not open his mouth.*

Officiant By oppression and judgment he was taken away. And who can speak of his descendants? For he was cut off from the land of the living; for the transgression of my people he was stricken.

People He was assigned a grave with the wicked, and with the rich in his death, though he had done no violence, nor was any deceit in his mouth.

Officiant Yet it was the LORD's will to crush him and cause him to suffer, and though the LORD makes his life a guilt offering, he will see his offspring and prolong his days, and the will of the LORD will prosper in his hand.

People After the suffering of his soul, he will see the light of life and be satisfied; by his knowledge my righteous servant will justify many, and he will bear their iniquities. Therefore I will give him a portion among the great, and he will divide the spoils with the strong, because he poured out his life unto death, and was numbered with the transgressors. For he bore the sin of many, and made intercession for the transgressors. [2]

A Hymn of Waiting

"In Silence my soul is waiting"

1. In   si - lence my soul   is   wait - ing,   Is   wait - ing for
2. You   set   on   a   man   and you beat   him,   The pack of   you
3. You   plot for his un - der - min - ing,   You slan - der him
4. Be   si - lent, my soul,   in   wait - ing,   In   wait - ing for
5. There's safe - ty in God,   and hon - or,   My   re - fuge, my
6. Just   puffs of the wind,   the peo - ple,   Great men are   il -
7. Don't   trust, then, in cruel ex - tor - tion,   Don't plun - der, de -
8. U -   nique - ly, our God   has spo - ken,   Of   two things I've

God a-lone, De-liv'-rance from Him is com-ing, My
knock him down, As a tot-ter-ing wall he stag-gers, Sub-
with your lies, You love, with faint praise, to damn him, Sweet
God a-lone, As-su-rance from Him is com-ing, My
rock, my strength, So hide in our God, you peo-ple, And
lu-sions, all, As breath in the air, they're mea-sured, Then
fraud and steal, Don't set your heart on pos-ses-sions, E-
heard Him speak— He's the source of pow'r and mer-cy, To

res-cu-er, fort and rock. In si-lence my soul is
sides like a sag-ging fence. In si-lence my soul is
tongued, you've a curse-filled heart. In si-lence my soul is
res-cu-er, fort and rock. Be si-lent, my soul, in
pour out your hearts to Him. Be si-lent, my soul, in
weight-less they fade a-way. Be si-lent, my soul, in
spe-cially if they in-crease. Be si-lent, my soul, in
men He re-pays their deeds. Be si-lent, my soul, in

wait-ing Se-cure, I shall not be moved.
wait-ing Se-cure, I shall not be moved.
wait-ing Se-cure, I shall not be moved.
wait-ing Se-cure, I shall not be moved.
wait-ing Se-cure, I shall not be moved.
wait-ing, Se-cure, I shall not be moved.
wait-ing, Se-cure, I shall not be moved.
wait-ing Se-cure, I shall not be moved.

Words: Michael Seward; Music: Christian Saward © 1973 The Jubilate
Group (Admin. Hope Publishing Company, Carol Stream, IL 60188).
All rights reserved. Used by permission.

A Reading from the Epistle of Paul to the Romans
[3:23-26; 5:6-8]

All have sinned and fall short of the glory of God, and are justified freely by his grace through the redemption that came by Christ Jesus. God presented him as a sacrifice of atonement, through faith in his blood. He did this to demonstrate his justice, because in his forbearance he had left the sins committed beforehand unpunished—he did it to demonstrate his justice at the present time, so as to be just and the one who justifies those who have faith in Jesus. . . .

You see, at just the right time, when we were still powerless, Christ died for the ungodly. Very rarely will anyone die for a righteous man, though for a good man someone might possibly dare to die. But God demonstrates his own love for us in this: While we were still sinners, Christ died for us. [3]

Hymn

"Just as I am without One Plea"

Charlotte Elliott (1789-1871)

Henry Smart (1813-1879)
Misericordia 8 8 8 6

1. Just as I am, with - out one plea, But that Thy
2. Just as I am, and wait - ing not To rid my
3. Just as I am, tho' tossed a - bout With ma-ny a
4. Just as I am, poor, wretch - ed, blind, Sight, rich - es,
5. Just as I am, Thou wilt re - ceive, Wilt wel - come,
6. Just as I am, Thy love un - known Hath bro - ken
7. Just as I am, of that free love The breadth, length

blood was shed for me, And that Thou bid'st me
soul of one dark blot, To Thee, whose blood can
con - flict, ma-ny a doubt, Fight - ings with - in, and
heal - ing of the mind, Yea, all I need, in
par - don, cleanse, re - lieve; Be - cause Thy pro - mise
e - v'ry bar - rier down; Now to be Thine, yea
depth, the height to prove, Here for a sea - son

come to Thee, O Lamb of God I come!
cleanse each spot, O Lamb of God I come!
fears with - out, O Lamb of God I come!
Thee to find, O Lamb of God I come!
I be - lieve, O Lamb of God I come!
Thine a - lone, O Lamb of God I come!
then a - bove, O Lamb of God I come! A - men.

75

A Reading from the Holy Gospel of our Lord Jesus Christ According to Matthew [27:15-26]

Now it was the custom at the Feast to release a prisoner whom the people requested. A man called Barabbas was in prison with the insurrectionists who had committed murder in the uprising. The crowd came up and asked Pilate to do for them what he usually did.

"Do you want me to release to you the king of the Jews?" asked Pilate, knowing it was out of envy that the chief priests had handed Jesus over to him. But the chief priests stirred up the crowd to have Pilate release Barabbas instead. "What shall I do, then, with the one you call the king of the Jews?" Pilate asked them. "Crucify him!" they shouted. "Why? What crime has he committed?" asked Pilate.

But they shouted all the louder, "Crucify him!" Wanting to satisfy the crowd, Pilate released Barabbas to them. He had Jesus flogged, and handed him over to be crucified. [4]

The Psalm [22:1-30]   *Deus, Deus meus*

1   My God, my God, why have you forsaken me? *
     and are so far from my cry and from the words of
     my distress?

2   O my God, I cry in the daytime, but you do not
     answer; *
     by night as well, but I find no rest.

3   Yet you are the Holy One, *
     enthroned upon the praises of Israel.

4   Our forefathers put their trust in you; *
     they trusted, and you delivered them.

5   They cried out to you and were delivered; *
     they trusted in you and were not put to shame.

6   But as for me, I am a worm and no man, *
     scorned by all and despised by the people.

7   All who see me laugh me to scorn; *
     they curl their lips and wag their heads, saying,

8   "He trusted in the Lord; let him deliver him; *
     let him rescue him, if he delights in him."

9   Yet you are he who took me out of the womb, *
     and kept me safe upon my mother's breast.

10   I have been entrusted to you ever since I was born; *
     you were my God when I was still in my mother's
     womb.

11   Be not far from me, for trouble is near, *
     and there is none to help.

12   Many young bulls encircle me; *
     strong bulls of Bashan surround me.

13   They open wide their jaws at me, *
     like a ravening and a roaring lion.

14   I am poured out like water;
     all my bones are out of joint; *
     my heart within my breast is melting wax.

15 My mouth is dried out like a pot-sherd;
    my tongue sticks to the roof of my mouth; *
    and you have laid me in the dust of the grave.

16 Packs of dogs close me in,
    and gangs of evildoers circle around me; *
    they pierce my hands and my feet;
    I can count all my bones.

17 They stare and gloat over me; *
    they divide my garments among them;
    they cast lots for my clothing.

18 Be not far away, O Lord; *
    you are my strength; hasten to help me.

19 Save me from the sword, *
    my life from the power of the dog.

20 Save me from the lion's mouth, *
    my wretched body from the horns of wild bulls.

21 I will declare your Name to my brethren; *
    in the midst of the congregation I will praise you.

22 Praise the Lord, you that fear him; *
    stand in awe of him, O offspring of Israel;
    all you of Jacob's line, give glory.

23 For he does not despise nor abhor the poor in their
    poverty; neither does he hide his face from them; *
    but when they cry to him he hears them.

24 My praise is of him in the great assembly; *
    I will perform my vows in the presence of those who
    worship him.

25 The poor shall eat and be satisfied,
and those who seek the Lord shall praise him: *
"May your heart live for ever!"

26 All the ends of the earth shall remember and turn to
the Lord, *
and all the families of the nations shall bow before
him.

27 For kingship belongs to the Lord; *
he rules over the nations.

28 To him alone all who sleep in the earth bow down
in worship; *
all who go down to the dust fall before him.

29 My soul shall live for him;
my descendants shall serve him; *
they shall be known as the Lord's for ever.

30 They shall come and make known to a people yet
unborn*
the saving deeds that he has done.

[Turn the page for the Hymn, *"Go to Dark Gethsemane"*]

Hymn

"Go to Dark Gethsemane"

1 Go to dark Geth - se - ma - ne, ye that feel the tempt-er's power;
2 Fol - low to the judg - ment hall; view the Lord of life ar-raigned;
3 Cal-vary's mourn-ful moun-tain climb; there, a - dor-ing at his feet,

your Re-deem-er's con-flict see, watch with him one bit - ter hour;
O the worm-wood and the gall! O the pangs his soul sus-tained!
mark the mir - a - cle of time, God's own sac - ri - fice com-plete;

turn not from his griefs a - way, learn of Je - sus Christ to pray.
Shun not suf - fering, shame, or loss; learn of him to bear the cross.
"It is fi - nished!" hear him cry; learn of Je - sus Christ to die.

Words: James Montgomery (1771-1854)
Music: *Petra*, Richard Redhead (1820-1901)

77. 77. 77

80

Celebrant Lord Jesus, all this for us? the jeering crowd, the crown of thorns, the nails driven through your hands and feet? the spitting, the insults, the tears. How great your love must be, love that led you to pay such a price for a cosmos gone wild. Give us eyes to see the immensity of Christ as Victor over all evil, natural and moral; over all human wickedness; and as judge and destroyer of principalities and powers. May we see you, Lord Christ, as the reigning King of Peace in a Kingdom that has come, is coming, and will come, to the glory of your Name. *Amen.*

A Reading from the Epistle of Paul to the Philippians
[2:6-8]

Jesus, being in very nature God did not consider equality with God something to be grasped, but made himself nothing, taking the very nature of a servant, being made in human likeness. And being found in appearance as a man, he humbled himself and became obedient to death even death on a cross! [5]

[Turn the page for the Hymn, *O Sacred Head Now Wounded"*]

Hymn

"O Sacred Head Now Wounded"

Authorship uncertain
Tr. by PAUL GERHARDT, 1607–1676
Tr. by JAMES W. ALEXANDER, 1804–1859

HANS L. HASSLER, 1564–1612
Harmonized by J. S. BACH, 1685–1750

1. O sa - cred Head, now wound - ed, With grief and shame weighed down,
2. What Thou, my Lord, hast suf - fered Was all for sin - ners' gain:
3. What lan - guage shall I bor - row To thank Thee, dear - est Friend,

Now scorn - ful - ly sur - round - ed With thorns, Thine on - ly crown;
Mine, mine was the trans - gres - sion, But Thine the dead - ly pain.
For this Thy dy - ing sor - row, Thy pit - y with - out end?

How pale Thou art with an - guish, With sore a - buse and scorn!
Lo, here I fall, my Sav - iour! 'Tis I de - serve Thy place;
O make me Thine for ev - er; And should I faint - ing be,

How does that vis - age lan - guish Which once was bright as morn!
Look on me with Thy fa - vor, Vouch - safe to me Thy grace.
Lord, let me nev - er, nev - er Out - live my love to Thee. A - MEN.

82

A Reading from the Holy Gospel of our Lord Jesus Christ According to John [17:1-5; 24-26]

Jesus looked toward heaven and prayed: "Father, the time has come. Glorify your Son, that your Son may glorify you. For you granted him authority over all people that he might give eternal life to all those you have given him. Now this is eternal life: that they may know you, the only true God, and Jesus Christ, whom you have sent. I have brought you glory on earth by completing the work you gave me to do. And now, Father, glorify me in your presence with the glory I had with you before the world began. "Father, I want those you have given me to be with me where I am, and to see my glory, the glory you have given me because you loved me before the creation of the world. Righteous Father, though the world does not know you, I know you, and they know that you have sent me. I have made you known to them, and will continue to make you known in order that the love you have for me may be in them and that I myself may be in them." [6]

A Reading from the Holy Gospel of Our Lord Jesus Christ According to Matthew [27:45-54]

From the sixth hour until the ninth hour darkness came over all the land. About the ninth hour Jesus cried out in a loud voice, "Eloi, Eloi, lama sabachthani?"—which means, "My God, my God, why have you forsaken me?" When some of those standing there heard this, they said, "He's calling Elijah." Immediately one of them ran and got a sponge. He filled it with wine vinegar, put it on a stick, and offered it to Jesus to drink. The rest said, "Now leave him alone. Let's see if Elijah comes to save him."

And when Jesus had cried out again in a loud voice, he gave up his spirit. At that moment the curtain of the temple was torn in two from top to bottom. The earth shook and the rocks split.++

The tombs broke open and the bodies of many holy people who had died were raised to life. They came out of the tombs, and after Jesus' resurrection they went into the holy city and appeared to many people.

When the centurion and those with him who were guarding Jesus saw the earthquake and all that had happened, they were terrified, and exclaimed, "Surely he was the Son of God!" [7]

A Hymn

"What Wondrous Love Is This?"

this	that	caused	the	Lord	of	bliss	to	bear	the dread-ful	curse	for	my
down	be -	neath	God's	righ-teous	frown,	Christ	laid	a -	side	His	crown	for	my
Lamb	Who	is	the	great	"I	Am,"	while	mil-lions join the theme, I	will
free	I'll	sing	and	joy -	ful	be;	and	through e - ter - ni - ty, I'll	sing

soul,	for	my	soul,	to	bear the dread-ful curse for my	soul.
soul,	for	my	soul,	Christ	laid a - side His crown for my	soul.
sing,	I	will	sing;	while	mil-lions join the theme, I will	sing.
on,	I'll	sing	on;	and	through e - ter - ni - ty, I'll sing	on.

WORDS: Stith Mead's *General Selection*, 1811
MUSIC: William Walker's *Southern Harmony*, 2nd ed., 1840; arr. William J. Reynolds, 1975

WONDROUS LOVE
12.9.12.12.9

A Reading from the Holy Gospel of our Lord Jesus Christ According to John [1:1-14]

In the beginning was the Word, and the Word was with God, and the Word was God. He was in the beginning with God. All things were made through him, and without him was not any thing made that was made. In him was life, and the life was the light of men. The light shines in the darkness, and the darkness has not overcome it.

There was a man sent from God, whose name was John. He came as a witness, to bear witness about the light, that all might believe through him. He was not the light, but came to bear witness about the light. The true light, which enlightens everyone, was coming into the world. He was in the world, and the world was made through him, yet the world did not know him. He came to his own, and his own people did not receive him. But to all who did receive him, who believed in his name, he gave the right to become children of God, who were born, not of blood nor of the will of the flesh nor of the will of man, but of God.

And the Word became flesh and dwelt among us, and we have seen his glory, glory as of the only Son from the Father, full of grace and truth. [8]

A Hymn

"Worthy is the Lamb"

1. "Wor-thy is the Lamb," the hosts of heav-en sing, As be-fore the
2. Wor-thy is the Lamb who shed His pre-cious blood To re-store a
3. Wor-thy is the Lamb, the bleed-ing sac-ri-fice, Who for A-dam's
4. "Wor-thy is the Lamb," let men and an-gels sing; "Wor-thy is the

throne they make His prais-es ring; "Wor-thy is the Lamb the
world to hap-pi-ness and God; When no eye could pit-y
race paid such a fear-ful price; Wor-thy is the Lamb, the
Lamb," let hal-le-lu-jahs ring; And when life is past, up-

book to o-pen wide; Wor-thy is the Lamb who once was cru-ci-fied."
and no arm could save, Je-sus, for our ran-som, Him-self free-ly gave.
pas-chal Lamb of God, For the world re-ceived re-demp-tion through His blood.
on the gold-en shore, "Wor-thy is the Lamb," we'll shout for-ev-er-more.

REFRAIN

Oh, this bleed-ing Lamb, oh, this bleed-ing Lamb, Oh, this dy-ing Lamb, He was found wor-thy; Oh, this bleed-ing Lamb, oh, this bleed-ing Lamb, Oh, this dy-ing Lamb, He was found wor-thy!

After the singing of the closing Hymn, the Christ candle is returned to its rightful place and we depart in the hope of the resurrection of the One who is the Light of the world.

Celebrant   Go in peace.
People   *In the Name of Christ. Amen.*

The

Maundy Thursday

Service from The

Book of Common Prayer

This service is found in the 1979 Book of Common Prayer, pages are noted for those who wish to follow. Other rubrics for **The Ceremony of Foot Washing** *may be found in* **"The Book of Occasional Services,"** *2003, page 93 ff.*

The Liturgy of the Word

The Prelude

The Processional Hymn

"Go to Dark Gethsemane"

1 Go to dark Gethsemane, ye that feel the tempt-er's power;
2 Fol-low to the judg-ment hall; view the Lord of life ar-raigned;
3 Cal-vary's mourn-ful moun-tain climb; there, a-dor-ing at his feet,

your Re-deem-er's con-flict see, watch with him one bit-ter hour;
O the worm-wood and the gall! O the pangs his soul sus-tained!
mark the mir-a-cle of time, God's own sac-ri-fice com-plete;

turn not from his griefs a-way, learn of Je-sus Christ to pray.
Shun not suf-fering, shame, or loss; learn of him to bear the cross.
"It is fi-nished!" hear him cry; learn of Je-sus Christ to die.

Words: James Montgomery (1771-1854)
Music: *Petra*, Richard Redhead (1820-1901)

♩=48
77. 77. 77

The Opening Acclamation

Celebrant   Bless the Lord who forgives all our sins.
People   *His mercy endures for ever.*

The Collect for Purity

Almighty God, to you all hearts are open, all desires known, and from you no secrets are hid: Cleanse the thoughts of our hearts by the inspiration of your Holy Spirit, that we may perfectly love you, and worthily magnify your holy Name; through Christ our Lord. Amen.

The Trisagion

[repeated three times]

Celebrant   Holy God,
                  Holy and Mighty,
                  Holy Immortal One,
People   *Have mercy upon us.*

The Collect of the Day

Celebrant   Almighty Father, whose dear Son, on the night before he suffered, instituted the Sacrament of his Body and Blood: Mercifully grant that we may receive it thankfully in remembrance of Jesus Christ our Lord, who in these holy mysteries gives us a pledge of eternal life; and who now lives and reigns with you and the Holy Spirit, one God, for ever and ever. Amen.

The Lessons

A Reading from the Book of Exodus [12:1-14a]

The LORD said to Moses and Aaron in the land of Egypt: This month shall mark for you the beginning of months; it shall be the first month of the year for you. Tell the whole congregation of Israel that on the tenth of this month they are to take a lamb for each family, a lamb for each household. If a household is too small for a whole lamb, it shall join its closest neighbor in obtaining one; the lamb shall be divided in proportion to the number of people who eat of it. [Your lamb shall be without blemish, a year-old male; you may take it from the sheep or from the goats. You shall keep it until the fourteenth day of this month; then the whole assembled congregation of Israel shall slaughter it at twilight. They shall take some of the blood and put it on the two doorposts and the lintel of the houses in which they eat it. They shall eat the lamb that same night; they shall eat it roasted over the fire with unleavened bread and bitter herbs. Do not eat any of it raw or boiled in water, but roasted over the fire, with its head, legs, and inner organs. You shall let none of it remain until the morning; anything that remains until the morning you shall burn.] This is how you shall eat it: your loins girded, your sandals on your feet, and your staff in your hand; and you shall eat it hurriedly. It is the passover of the LORD. For I will pass through the land of Egypt that night, and I will strike down every firstborn in the land of Egypt, both human beings and animals; on all the gods of Egypt I will execute judgments: I am the LORD. The blood shall be a sign for you on the houses where you live: when I see the blood, I will pass over you, and no plague shall destroy you when I strike the land of Egypt.

This day shall be a day of remembrance for you. You shall celebrate it as a festival to the LORD; throughout your generations you shall observe it as a perpetual ordinance.

Lector The Word of the Lord
People *Thanks be to God.*

The Psalm [78:14-20; 23-25]

14   He led them with a cloud by day, *
        and all the night through with a glow of fire.

15   He split the hard rocks in the wilderness *
        and gave them drink as from the great deep.

16   He brought streams out of the cliff, *
        and the waters gushed out like rivers.

17   But they went on sinning against him, *
        rebelling in the desert against the Most High.

18   They tested God in their hearts, *
        demanding food for their craving.

19   They railed against God and said, *
        "Can God set a table in the wilderness?

20   True, he struck the rock, the waters gushed out,
        and the gullies overflowed; *
        but is he able to give bread or to provide meat for
        his people?

21   When the Lord heard this, he was full of wrath; *
        a fire was kindled against Jacob, and his anger
        mounted against Israel;

22   For they had no faith in God, *
        nor did they put their trust in his saving power.

23   So he commanded the clouds above *
        and opened the doors of heaven.

24   He rained down manna upon them to eat *
        and gave them grain from heaven.

25   So mortals ate the bread of angels; *
        he provided for them food enough.

A Reading from the First Epistle of Paul to the Corinthians [11:23-26]

For I received from the Lord what I also handed on to you, that the Lord Jesus on the night when he was betrayed took a loaf of bread, and when he had given thanks, he broke it and said, "This is my body that is for you. Do this in remembrance of me." In the same way he took the cup also, after supper, saying, "This cup is the new covenant in my blood. Do this, as often as you drink it, in remembrance of me." For as often as you eat this bread and drink the cup, you proclaim the Lord's death until he comes.

Lector   The Word of the Lord
People   *Thanks be to God.*

The Sequence Hymn

"Ah, Holy Jesus, How hast Thou Offended?"

1 Ah, ho-ly Je-sus, how hast thou of-fend-ed, that man to
2 Who was the guilt-y? Who brought this up-on thee? A-las, my
3 Lo, the Good Shep-herd for the sheep is of-fered; the slave hath
4 For me, kind Je-sus, was thy in-car-na-tion, thy mor-tal
5 There-fore, kind Je-sus, since I can-not pay thee, I do a-

1 judge thee hath in hate pre-tend-ed? By foes de-rid-ed,
2 trea-son, Je-sus, hath un-done thee. 'Twas I, Lord Je-sus,
3 sin-ned, and the Son hath suf-fered; for our a-tone-ment,
4 sor-row, and thy life's ob-la-tion; thy death of an-guish
5 dore thee, and will ev-er pray thee, think on thy pi-ty

1 by thine own re-ject-ed, O most af-flict-ed.
2 I it was de-nied thee: I cru-ci-fied thee.
3 while we noth-ing heed-ed, God in-ter-ced-ed.
4 and thy bit-ter pas-sion, for my sal-va-tion.
5 and thy love un-swerv-ing, not my de-serv-ing.

Words: Johann Heermann (1585-1647); tr. Robert Seymour Bridges (1844-1930)
Music: *Herzliebster Jesu,* Johann Cruger (1598-1662), alt.

♩=52
11 11. 11 5

Deacon   **The Holy Gospel of our Lord Jesus Christ**
         According to John [13:1-17, 31b-35]
People   *Glory to you, Lord Christ.*

Now before the festival of the Passover, Jesus knew that his hour had come to depart from this world and go to the Father. Having loved his own who were in the world, he loved them to the end. The devil had already put it into the heart of Judas son of Simon Iscariot to betray him. And during supper Jesus, knowing that the Father had given all things into his hands, and that he had come from God and was going to God, got up from the table, took off his outer robe, and tied a towel around himself. Then he poured water into a basin and began to wash the disciples' feet and to wipe them with the towel that was tied around him. He came to Simon Peter, who said to him, "Lord, are you going to wash my feet?" Jesus answered, "You do not know now what I am doing, but later you will understand." Peter said to him, "You will never wash my feet." Jesus answered, "Unless I wash you, you have no share with me." Simon Peter said to him, "Lord, not my feet only but also my hands and my head!" Jesus said to him, "One who has bathed does not need to wash, except for the feet, but is entirely clean. And you are clean, though not all of you." For he knew who was to betray him; for this reason he said, "Not all of you are clean."

After he had washed their feet, had put on his robe, and had returned to the table, he said to them, "Do you know what I have done to you? You call me Teacher and Lord—and you are right, for that is what I am. So if I, your Lord and Teacher, have washed your feet, you also ought to wash one another's feet. For I have set you an example, that you also should do as I have done to you. Very truly, I tell you, servants are not greater than their master, nor are messengers greater than the one who sent them. If you know these things, you are blessed if you do them.

Jesus said, "Now the Son of Man has been glorified, and God has been glorified in him. If God has been glorified in him, God will also glorify him in himself and will glorify him at once. Little children, I am with you only a little longer. You will look for me; and as I said to the Jews so now I say to you, 'Where I am going, you cannot come.' I give you a new commandment, that you love one another. Just as I have loved you, you also should love one another. By this everyone will know that you are my disciples, if you have love for one another."

Deacon   The Gospel of the Lord.
People   *Praise to you, Lord Christ.*

The Homily

The Ceremony of Foot Washing

Bishops, priests, and deacons wash the feet of people of the congregation. Following this members of the congregation are invited to wash each others feet. No one is required to participate. If you do not participate in the foot washing, please participate by joining in the singing of hymns.

Sequence Hymn One

"There is Healing at the Fountain"

Fanny J. Crosby, 1820-1915   William J. Kirkpatrick, 1838-1921

1. There is heal-ing at the foun-tain, Come, be-hold the crim-son tide,
2. There is heal-ing at the foun-tain, Come and find it, wea-ry soul,
3. There is heal-ing at the foun-tain, Look to Je-sus now and live,
4. There is heal-ing at the foun-tain, Pre-cious foun-tain filled with blood;

Flow - ing down from Cal-vary's moun-tain, Where the Prince of Glo-ry died.
There your sins may all be cov-ered; Je - sus waits to make you whole.
At the cross lay down thy bur - den; All thy wan-derings He'll for - give.
Come, oh come, the Sav-iour calls you, Come and plunge be-neath its flood.

REFRAIN

Oh, the foun-tain! Bless-ed heal-ing foun-tain! I am glad 'tis flow-ing free;

Oh, the foun-tain! Pre-cious, cleans-ing foun-tain! Praise the Lord, it cleans-eth me.

Sequence Hymn Two [if needed]

[It is suggested that since this Hymn is a prayer, that the "Amen" be included at end of the final stanza]

"When this Passing world is done"

Robert M. McCheyne, 1813-1843

Richard Redhead, 1820-1901

1. When this pass-ing world is done, When has sunk yon glar-ing sun,
2. When I stand be - fore the throne, Dressed in beau-ty not my own,
3. When the praise of heaven I hear, Loud as thun-ders to the ear,
4. Even on earth, as through a glass, Dark-ly, let Thy glo-ry pass;

When I stand with Christ in glo-ry, Look-ing o'er life's fin - ished sto-ry—
When I see Thee as Thou art, Love Thee with un-sin - ning heart—
Loud as man-y wa-ters' noise, Sweet as harp's me-lo - dious voice—
Make for-give-ness feel so sweet; Make Thy Spir - it's help so meet—

Then, Lord, shall I ful - ly know, Not till then, how much I owe.
Then, Lord, shall I ful - ly know, Not till then, how much I owe.
Then, Lord, shall I ful - ly know, Not till then, how much I owe.
Even on earth, Lord, make me know Some-thing of how much I owe. A-MEN.

100

The Nicene Creed *all stand*

We believe in one God,
    the Father, the Almighty,
    maker of heaven and earth,
    of all that is, seen and unseen.

We believe in one Lord, Jesus Christ,
    the only Son of God,
    eternally begotten of the Father,
    God from God, Light from Light,
    true God from true God,
    begotten, not made, of one Being with the Father.
  Through him all things were made.
  For us and for our salvation
     he came down from heaven:
  by the power of the Holy Spirit
      he became incarnate from the Virgin Mary,
      and was made man.
For our sake he was crucified under Pontius Pilate;
    he suffered death and was buried.
  On the third day he rose again
     in accordance with the Scriptures;
  he ascended into heaven
     and is seated at the right hand of the Father.
He will come again in glory to judge the living and the
  dead, and his kingdom will have no end.

We believe in the Holy Spirit, the Lord, the giver of life,
    who proceeds from the Father and the Son.
    With the Father and the Son he is worshiped and
  glorified. He has spoken through the Prophets.
We believe in one holy catholic and apostolic Church.
    We acknowledge one baptism for the forgiveness of
    sins.
    We look for the resurrection of the dead,
     and the life of the world to come. Amen.

The Prayers of the People *all kneel*

Father, we pray for your holy Catholic Church;
That we all may be one.

Grant that every member of the Church may truly and humbly serve you;
That your Name may be glorified by all people.

We pray for all bishops, priests, and deacons;
That they may be faithful ministers of your Word and Sacraments.

We pray for all who govern and hold authority in the nations of the world;
That there may be justice and peace on the earth.

Give us grace to do your will in all that we undertake;
That our works may find favor in your sight.

Have compassion on those who suffer from any grief or trouble;
That they may be delivered from their distress.

Give to the departed eternal rest;
Let light perpetual shine upon them.

We praise you for your saints who have entered into joy;
May we also come to share in your heavenly kingdom.

Let us name before God those for whom we offer our various prayers this night.

Celebrant O Lord our God, accept the fervent prayers of your people; in the multitude of your mercies, look with compassion upon us and all who turn to you for help; for you are gracious, O lover of souls, and to you we give glory, Father, Son, and Holy Spirit, now and for ever. *Amen.*

The Confession of Sin & Absolution

Celebrant and People

Most merciful God,
we confess that we have sinned against you
in thought, word, and deed,
by what we have done,
and by what we have left undone.
We have not loved you with our whole heart;
we have not loved our neighbors as ourselves.
We are truly sorry and we humbly repent.
For the sake of your Son Jesus Christ,
have mercy on us and forgive us;
that we may delight in your will,
and walk in your ways,
to the glory of your Name. Amen.

The Priest stands and says

Almighty God have mercy on you, forgive you all your
sins through our Lord Jesus Christ, strengthen you in all
goodness, and by the power of the Holy Spirit keep you in
eternal life. *Amen.*

The Peace

Celebrant   The peace of the Lord be always with you.
People   And also with you.

The Holy Eucharist

The Offertory & Hymn

"My Faith looks up to Thee"

1. My faith looks up to Thee, Thou Lamb of Cal - va - ry, Sav - ior di - vine. Now hear me while I pray, Take all my guilt a - way. O, let me from this day Be whol - ly Thine!

2. May Thy rich grace im - part Strength to my faint - ing heart, My zeal in - spire. As Thou hast died for me, O, may my love to Thee Pure, warm, and change - less be, A liv - ing fire!

3. While life's dark maze I tread And griefs a - round me spread, Be Thou my guide. Bid dark - ness turn to day, Wipe sor - row's tears a - way, Nor let me ev - er stray From Thee a - side.

4. When ends life's tran - sient dream, When death's cold, sul - len stream Shall o'er me roll, Blest Sav - ior, then, in love, Fear and dis - trust re - move. O, bear me safe a - bove, A ran - somed soul!

WORDS: Ray Palmer, 1808-1887
MUSIC: Lowell Mason, 1792-1872

OLIVET
6.6.4.6.6.6.4.

The Doxology *all stand*

Praise God from whom all blessings flow;
Praise him all creatures here, below.
Praise him above, ye heavenly hosts.
Praise Father, Son, and Holy Ghost. Amen.

The people remain standing.

The Sursum Corda

Celebrant The Lord be with you.
People   And also with you.
Celebrant   Lift up your hearts.
People   We lift them to the Lord.
Celebrant Let us give thanks to the Lord our God.
People   It is right to give him thanks and praise.

The Celebrant

It is right, and a good and joyful thing, always and
everywhere to give thanks to you, Father Almighty,
Creator of heaven and earth.

Therefore we praise you, joining our voices with Angels
and Archangels and with all the company of heaven, who
for ever sing this Hymn to proclaim the glory of your
Name

Celebrant and People

Holy, holy, holy Lord, God of power and might,
heaven and earth are full of your glory.
    Hosanna in the highest.
Blessed is he who comes in the name of the Lord.
    Hosanna in the highest.

The people kneel [sit if you need to so do]

Then the Celebrant continues

Holy and gracious Father: In your infinite love you made us for yourself; and, when we had fallen into sin and become subject to evil and death, you, in your mercy, sent Jesus Christ, your only and eternal Son, to share our human nature, to live and die as one of us, to reconcile us to you, the God and Father of all.

He stretched out his arms upon the cross, and offered himself, in obedience to your will, a perfect sacrifice for the whole world.

On the night he was handed over to suffering and death, our Lord Jesus Christ took bread; and when he had given thanks to you, he broke it, and gave it to his disciples, and said, "Take, eat: This is my Body, which is given for you. Do this for the remembrance of me."

After supper he took the cup of wine; and when he had given thanks, he gave it to them, and said, "Drink this, all of you: This is my Blood of the new Covenant, which is shed for you and for many for the forgiveness of sins. Whenever you drink it, do this for the remembrance of me." Therefore we proclaim the mystery of faith:

Celebrant and People

Christ has died.
Christ is risen.
Christ will come again.

The Celebrant continues

We celebrate the memorial of our redemption, O Father, in this sacrifice of praise and thanksgiving.

Recalling his death, resurrection, and ascension, we offer you these gifts.

Sanctify them by your Holy Spirit to be for your people the Body and Blood of your Son, the holy food and drink of new and unending life in him. Sanctify us also that we may faithfully receive this holy Sacrament, and serve you in unity, constancy, and peace; and at the last day bring us with all your saints into the joy of your eternal kingdom.

All this we ask through your Son Jesus Christ. By him, and with him, and in him, in the unity of the Holy Spirit all honor and glory is yours, Almighty Father, now and for ever. *AMEN.*

And now, as our Savior Christ has taught us, we are bold to say,

People and Celebrant

Our Father, who art in heaven,
  hallowed be thy Name,
  thy kingdom come,
  thy will be done,
    on earth as it is in heaven.
Give us this day our daily bread.
And forgive us our trespasses,
 as we forgive those
  who trespass against us.
And lead us not into temptation,
 but deliver us from evil.
For thine is the kingdom,
 and the power, and the glory,
 for ever and ever. Amen.

The Breaking of the Bread

The Celebrant Christ our Passover is sacrificed for us;
The People *Therefore let us keep the feast.*

The Invitation to Communion

The Celebrant The Gifts of God for the People of God.
Take them in remembrance that Christ died for you, and
feed on him in your hearts by faith, with thanksgiving

Communion Music

"There is a Fountain Filled with Blood""

1. There   is   a   foun-tain filled with   blood Drawn from Im - man - uel's   veins,
2. The   dy - ing thief re - joiced   to   see   That   foun-tain   in   his   day,
3. *Dear   dy - ing Lamb, Thy   pre - cious   blood   Shall   nev - er   lose   its   power,*
4. E'er   since, by faith, I   saw   the   stream Thy   flow-ing wounds sup - ply,
5. When   this poor lisp-ing, stam-mering tongue Lies   si - lent   in   the   grave,

And   sin - ners plunged be - neath that flood   Lose   all   their guilt - y   stains:
And   there may   I,   though   vile   as   he,   Wash   all   my   sins a - way:
Till   all   the   ran - somed Church of   God   Be   saved, to   sin   no   more:
Re - deem-ing love   has   been   my theme And   shall   be   till   I   die:
Then   in   a   no - bler,   sweet - er   song   I'll   sing Thy power to   save:

Lose all their guilt-y stains, Lose all their guilt-y stains;
Wash all my sins a-way, Wash all my sins a-way;
Be saved, to sin no more, Be saved, to sin no more;
And shall be till I die, And shall be till I die;
I'll sing Thy power to save, I'll sing Thy power to save;

And sin-ners plunged be-neath that flood Lose all their guilt-y stains.
And there may I, though vile as he, Wash all my sins a-way.
Till all the ran-somed Church of God Be saved, to sin no more.
Re-deem-ing love has been my theme And shall be till I die.
Then in a no-bler, sweet-er song I'll sing Thy power to save.

The Postcommunion Prayer

Celebrant and People

Eternal God, heavenly Father,
you have graciously accepted us as living members
of your Son our Savior Jesus Christ,
and you have fed us with spiritual food
in the Sacrament of his Body and Blood.
Send us now into the world in peace,
and grant us strength and courage
to love and serve you
with gladness and singleness of heart;
through Christ our Lord. Amen.

The Blessing

The Processional Hymn

"In Remembrance of Thee"

1. In re - mem - brance of Thee do we gath - er to - day, 'Round Thy
2. Here a ta - ble is spread of for - give - ness and grace, Here our
3. There He drank of the cup of our sin and our death, Let us
4. When He comes for His Church what a joy it will be To par-

ta - ble of mer - cy so free. For as oft as we eat, and as
needs and our wants He doth meet. He took bread and gave thanks, and He
come and for - give - ness re - ceive Through His blood which was shed for re -
take of the cup from His hand. We will sit at His feet as we

oft as we drink, Do we come in re - mem - brance of Thee.
broke it for them, He said: "Take of my bod - y and eat."
mis - sion of sin, Let us come, eat and drink and be - lieve.
wor - ship our Lord, From all tongues and all tribes and all lands.

Final Ending

In re - mem-brance of Thee, We do show the Lord's death till He come.

The Dismissal – *People Respond* Thanks be to God.

The

Book of Common Prayer

Service

for

Good Friday

"The Mass of the Pre-sanctified"

The Ministers enter in Silence

All then kneel for silent prayer, after which the Celebrant stands and begins the liturgy with the Collect of the Day.

The Collect for Good Friday

Celebrant   Blessed be our God.
People   For ever and ever. Amen.
Celebrant   Let us pray.

Almighty God, we pray you graciously to behold this your family, for whom our Lord Jesus Christ was willing to be betrayed, and given into the hands of sinners, and to suffer death upon the cross; who now lives and reigns with you and the Holy Spirit, one God, for ever and ever. *Amen.*

The Holy Scriptures

Old Testament Isaiah [52:13—53:12]
Psalm   [22:1-21]
Epistle Hebrews [10:1-25]

Celebrant   The Passion of our Lord Jesus Christ according to John [18:1—19:37]

The congregation remains seated for the first part of the Passion Gospel. At the verse which mentions the arrival at Golgotha (John 19:17) all stand.

The Passion Narrative according to the Gospel of John [18:1-19:37]

READER ONE: When Jesus had spoken these words, he went forth with his disciples across the Kidron valley, where there was a garden, which he and his disciples entered. Now Judas, who betrayed him, also knew the place; for Jesus often met there with his disciples. So Judas, procuring a band of soldiers and some officers from the chief priests and the Pharisees, went there with lanterns and torches and weapons. Then Jesus, knowing all that was to befall him, came forward and said to them, "Whom do you seek?" They answered him, "Jesus of Nazareth." Jesus said to them, "I am he." Judas, who betrayed him, was standing with them. When he said to them, "I am he," they drew back and fell to the ground. Again he asked them, "Whom do you seek?" And they said, "Jesus of Nazareth." Jesus answered, "I told you that I am he; so if you seek me, let these men go." This was to fulfil the word which he had spoken, "of those whom thou gavest me I lost not one." Then Simon Peter, having a sword, drew it and struck the high priest's slave and cut off his right ear. The slave's name was Malchus. Jesus said to Peter, "Put your sword into its sheath; shall I not drink the cup which the Father has given me?"

READER TWO: So the band of soldiers and their captain and the officers of the Jews seized Jesus and bound him. First they led him to Annas; for he was the father-in-law of Caiaphas, who was high priest that year. It was Caiaphas who had given counsel to the Jews that it was expedient that one man should die for the people.

READER THREE: Simon Peter followed Jesus, and so did another disciple. As this disciple was known to the high priest, he entered the court of the high priest along with Jesus, while Peter stood outside at the door. So the other disciple, who was known to the high priest, went out and spoke to the man who kept the door and brought Peter in. The maid who kept the door said to Peter, "Are not you also one of this man's disciples?" He said, "I am not."

Now the servants and the officers had made a charcoal fire, because it was cold, and they were standing and warming themselves; Peter also was with them, standing and warming himself.

READER FOUR: The high priest then questioned Jesus about his disciples and his teaching. Jesus answered him, "I have spoken openly to the world; I have always taught in the synagogues and in the temple, where all Jews come together; I have said nothing secretly. Why do you ask me? Ask those who have heard me, what I said to them; they know what I said." When he had said this, one of the officers standing by struck Jesus with his hand, saying, "Is that how you answer the high priest?" Jesus answered him, "If I have spoken wrongly, bear witness to the wrong; but if I have spoken rightly, why do you strike me?" Annas then sent him bound to Caiaphas the high priest.

READER FIVE: Now Simon Peter was standing and warming himself. They said to him, "Are not you also one of his disciples?" He denied it and said, "I am not." One of the servants of the high priest, a kinsman of the man whose ear Peter had cut off, asked, "Did I not see you in the garden with him?" Peter again denied it; and at once the cock crowed.

READER SIX: Then they led Jesus from the house of Caiaphas to the praetorium. It was early. They themselves did not enter the praetorium, so that they might not be defiled, but might eat the Passover. So Pilate went out to them and said, "What accusation do you bring against this man?" They answered him, "If this man were not an evildoer, we would not have handed him over." Pilate said to them, "Take him yourselves and judge him by your own law." The Jews said to him, "it is not lawful for us to put any man to death." This was to fulfil the word which Jesus had spoken to show by what death he was to die.

READER SEVEN: Pilate entered the praetorium again and called Jesus, and said to him, "Are you the King of the Jews?" Jesus answered, "do you say this of your own accord, or did others say it to you about me?" Pilate answered, "Am I a Jew?" Your own nation and the chief priests have handed you over to me; what have you done?" Jesus answered, "My kingship is not of this world; if my kingship were of this world, my servants would fight, that I might not be handed over to the Jews; but my kingship is not from the world." Pilate said to him, "So you are a king?" Jesus answered, "You say that I am a king. For this I was born, and for this I have come into the world, to bear witness to the truth. Every one who is of the truth hears my voice." Pilate said to him, "What is truth?"

READER EIGHT: After he had said this, he went out to the Jews again, and told them, "I find no crime in him. But you have a custom that I should release one man for you at the Passover; will you have me release for you the King of the Jews?" They cried out again, "Not this man, but Barabbas!" Now Barabbas was a robber.

READER NINE: When Pilate heard these words, he was the more afraid; he entered the praetorium again and said to Jesus, "Where are you from?" But Jesus gave no answer. Pilate therefore said to him, "You will not speak to me? Do you not know that I have power to release you, and power to crucify you?" Jesus answered him, "You would have no power over me unless it had been given you from above; therefore he who delivered me to you has the greater sin."

Upon this Pilate sought to release him, but the Jews cried out, "If you release this man, you are not Caesar's friend; everyone who makes himself a king sets himself against Caesar." When Pilate heard these words, he brought Jesus out and sat down on the judgment seat at a place called The Pavement, and in Hebrew, Gabbatha. Now it was the day of Preparation of the Passover; it was about the sixth hour. He said to the Jews, "Behold your King!" They cried out "Away with him, away with him, crucify him!" Pilate said to them, "Shall I crucify your king?" The chief priests answered, "We have no King but Caesar." Then he handed him over to them to be crucified.

READER TEN: So they took Jesus, and he went out, bearing his own cross, to the place called the place of a skull, which is called in Hebrew Golgotha. *[All stand]* There they crucified him, and with him two others, one on either side, and Jesus between them. Pilate also wrote a title and put it on the cross; it read, "Jesus of Nazareth, the King of the Jews." Many of the Jews read this title, for the place where Jesus was crucified was near the city; and it was written in Hebrew, in Latin, and in Greek. The chief priests of the Jews then said to Pilate, "Do not write, 'The King of the Jews,' but, 'This man said, I am the King of the Jews.'" Pilate answered, "What I have written I have written."

When the four soldiers had crucified Jesus they took his garments and made four parts, one for each soldier; also his tunic. But the tunic was without seam, woven from top to bottom; so they said to one another, "Let us not tear it, but cast lots for it to see whose it shall be." This was to fulfill the scripture, "They parted my garments among them, and for my clothing they cast lots." So the soldiers did this.

After this Jesus, knowing that all was finished, said (to fulfill the scripture), "I thirst." A bowl full of vinegar stood there; so they put a sponge full of the vinegar on hyssop and held it to his mouth. When Jesus had received the vinegar, he said, "It is finished": and he bowed his head and gave up his spirit.

READER ELEVEN: Since it was the day of Preparation, in order to prevent the bodies from remaining on the cross on the Sabbath (for that Sabbath was a high day), the Jews asked Pilate that their legs might be broken, and that they might be taken away. So the soldiers came and broke the legs of the first, and of the other who had been crucified with him: but when they came to Jesus and saw that he was already dead, they did not break his legs. But one of the soldiers pierced his side with a spear, and at once there came out blood and water. He who saw it has borne witness—his testimony is true, and he knows that he tells the truth—that you also may believe. For these things took place that the scripture might be fulfilled, "Not a bone of him shall be broken." And again another scripture says, "They shall look on him who they have pierced."

After this Joseph of Arimathea, who was a disciple of Jesus, but secretly, for fear of the Jews, asked Pilate that he might take away the body of Jesus, and Pilate gave him leave. So he came and took away his body. Nicodemus also, who had at first come to him by night, came bringing a mixture of myrrh and aloes, about a hundred pound's weight. They took the body of Jesus, and bound it in linen cloths with spices, as is the burial custom of the Jews. Now in the place where he was crucified there was a garden, and in the garden a new tomb where no one had ever been laid. So because of the Jewish day of Preparation, as the tomb was close at hand, they laid Jesus there.

The Homily

A Hymn

"Were You There When They Crucified My Lord?"

1 Were you there when they cru-ci-fied my Lord? Were you
2 Were you there when they nailed him to the tree? Were you
*3 Were you there when they pierced him in the side? Were you
4 Were you there when they laid him in the tomb? Were you

there when they cru-ci-fied my Lord? Oh!
there when they nailed him to the tree? Oh!
there when they pierced him in the side? Oh!
there when they laid him in the tomb? Oh!

Some-times it caus-es me to trem-ble, trem-ble,
Some-times it caus-es me to trem-ble, trem-ble,
Some-times it caus-es me to trem-ble, trem-ble,
Some-times it caus-es me to trem-ble, trem-ble,

trem-ble. Were you there when they cru-ci-fied my Lord?
trem-ble. Were you there when they nailed him to the tree?
trem-ble. Were you there when they pierced him in the side?
trem-ble. Were you there when they laid him in the tomb?

The Solemn Collects *All standing*

[Deacon or appointed Reader] Dear People of God: Our heavenly Father sent his Son into the world, not to condemn the world, but that the world through him might be saved; that all who believe in him might be delivered from the power of sin and death, and become heirs with him of everlasting life.

We pray, therefore, for people everywhere according to their needs. *The Celebrant and people kneel.*

The Celebrant prays the Collects.

Reader Let us pray for the holy Catholic Church of Christ throughout the world;

> For its unity in witness and service
> For all bishops and other ministers
> and the people whom they serve
> For *N.*, our Bishop, and all the people of this diocese
> For all Christians in this community
> For those about to be baptize (particularly_____)

That God will confirm his Church in faith, increase it in love, and preserve it in peace.

Silence

Celebrant Almighty and everlasting God, by whose Spirit the whole body of your faithful people is governed and sanctified: Receive our supplications and prayers which we offer before you for all members of your holy Church, that in their vocation and ministry they may truly and devoutly serve you; through our Lord and Savior Jesus Christ. *Amen.*

Reader Let us pray for all nations and peoples of the earth, and for those in authority among them;

> For _____, the President of the United States
> For our Governor and State Legislature
> For the Congress and the Supreme Court
> For the Members and Representatives of the United Nations
> For all who are called on to serve the common good

That by God's help they may seek justice and truth, and live in peace and concord.

Silence

Almighty God, kindle, we pray, in every heart the true love of peace, and guide with your wisdom those who take counsel for the nations of the earth; that in tranquility your dominion may increase, until the earth is filled with the knowledge of your love; through Jesus Christ our Lord. *Amen.*

Reader Let us pray for all who suffer and are afflicted in body or in mind;
> For the hungry and the homeless, the destitute and the oppressed
> For the sick, the wounded, and the crippled
> For those in loneliness, fear, and anguish
> For those who face temptation, doubt, and despair
> For the sorrowful and bereaved
> For prisoners and captives, and those in mortal danger

That God in his mercy will comfort and relieve them, and grant them the knowledge of his love, and stir up in us the will and patience to minister to their needs.

Silence

Celebrant Gracious God, the comfort of all who sorrow, the strength of all who suffer: Let the cry of those in misery and need come to you, that they may find your mercy present with them in all their afflictions; and give us, we pray, the strength to serve them for the sake of him who suffered for us, your Son Jesus Christ our Lord. *Amen.*

Reader Let us pray for all who have not received the Gospel of Christ;

> For those who have never heard the word of salvation
> For those who have lost their faith
> For those hardened by sin or indifference
> For the contemptuous and the scornful
> For those who are enemies of the cross of Christ and persecutors of his disciples
> For those who in the name of Christ have persecuted

others, that God will open their hearts to the truth, and lead them to faith and obedience.

Silence

Celebrant Merciful God, creator of all the peoples of the earth and lover of souls: Have compassion on all who do not know you as you are revealed in your Son Jesus Christ; let your Gospel be preached with grace and power to those who have not heard it; turn the hearts of those who resist it; and bring home to your fold those who have gone astray; that there may be one flock under one shepherd, Jesus Christ our Lord. *Amen.*

Reader Let us commit ourselves to our God, and pray for the grace of a holy life, that, with all who have departed this world and have died in the peace of Christ, and those whose faith is known to God alone, we may be accounted worthy to enter into the fullness of the joy of our Lord, and receive the crown of life in the day of resurrection.

Silence

Celebrant O God of unchangeable power and eternal light: Look favorably on your whole Church, that wonderful and sacred mystery; by the effectual working of your providence, carry out in tranquility the plan of salvation; let the whole world see and know that things which were cast down are being raised up, and things which had grown old are being made new, and that all things are being brought to their perfection by him through whom all things were made, your Son Jesus Christ our Lord; who lives and reigns with you, in the unity of the Holy Spirit, one God, for ever and ever. *Amen.*

A Hymn

"Stabat Mater"

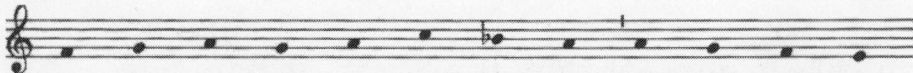

1 At the cross her vig - il keep - ing, stood the mourn - ful
2 With what pain and des - o - la - tion, with what grief and
3 Him she saw for our sal - va - tion mocked with cru - el
4 Who, on Christ's dear mo - ther gaz - ing, pierced by an - guish
5 Je - sus, may her deep de - vo - tion stir in me the

1 mo - ther weep - ing, where he hung, the dy - ing Lord:
2 res - ig - na - tion, Mar - y watched her dy - ing son.
3 ac - cla - ma - tion, scourged, and crowned with thorns en - twined;
4 so a - maz - ing, born of wo - man, would not weep?
5 same e - mo - tion, Fount of love, Re - deem - er kind;

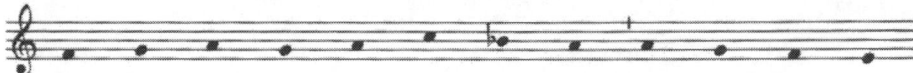

1 there she wait - ed in her an - guish, see - ing Christ in
2 Deep the woe of her af - flic - tion, when she saw the
3 saw him then from judg - ment tak - en, and in death by
4 Who, on Christ's dear mo - ther think - ing, such a cup of
5 that my heart fresh ar - dor gain - ing, and a pur - er

1 tor - ment lan - guish, in her heart the pierc - ing sword.
2 cru - ci - fi - xion of the sole - be - got - ten one.
3 all for - sak - en, till his spi - rit he re - signed.
4 sor - row drink - ing, would not share her sor - rows deep?
5 love at - tain - ing, may with thee ac - cept - ance find.

Anthem 1

Celebrant   We glory in your cross, O Lord,
People   *and praise and glorify your holy resurrection;*
                       for by virtue of your cross
                       joy has come to the whole world.

Celebrant   May God be merciful to us and bless us,
                       show us the light of his countenance, and
                       come to us.

People   *Let your ways be known upon earth,*
                       your saving health among all nations.

Celebrant   Let the peoples praise you, O God;
                       let all the peoples praise you.

People   *We glory in your cross, O Lord,*
                       and praise and glorify your holy resurrection;
                       for by virtue of your cross
                       joy has come to the whole world.

Anthem 2

Celebrant   We adore you, O Christ, and we bless you,
People   *because by your holy cross you have redeemed*
               the world.

Celebrant   If we have died with him, we shall also live
                       with him; if we endure, we shall also reign
                       with him.

People   *We adore you, O Christ, and we bless you,*
                   because by your holy cross you have redeemed
                   the world.

Anthem 3

Celebrant   O Savior of the world, who by thy cross and
precious blood hast redeemed us:

People   *Save us and help us, we humbly beseech thee, O
Lord.*

A Hymn

"Sing, my Tongue, the Glorious Battle"

[Stanza lines — first staff]

1 Sing, my tongue, the glo-rious bat - tle; of the might - y con - flict
2 Thir - ty years a - mong us dwell - ing, his ap - point - ed time ful -
3 He en - dures the nails, the spit - ting, vin - e - gar, and spear, and
4 Faith - ful cross! a - bove all o - ther, one and on - ly no - ble
5 Bend thy boughs, O tree of glo - ry! Thy re - lax - ing sin - ews
*6 Praise and hon - or to the Fa - ther, praise and hon - or to the

[Second staff]

1 sing; tell the tri - umph of the vic - tim, to his
2 filled, born for this, he meets his pas - sion, this the
3 reed; from that ho - ly bo - dy bro - ken blood and
4 tree! None in fo - liage, none in blos - som, none in
5 bend; for a - while the an - cient ri - gor that thy
6 Son, praise and hon - or to the Spi - rit, ev - er

[Third staff]

1 cross thy tri - bute bring. Je - sus Christ, the world's Re -
2 Sa - vior free - ly willed: on the cross the Lamb is
3 wa - ter forth pro - ceed: earth, and stars, and sky, and
4 fruit thy peer may be: sweet - est wood and sweet - est
5 birth be - stowed, sus - pend; and the King of heaven - ly
6 Three and ev - er One: one in might and one in

[Fourth staff]

1 deem - er from that cross now reigns as King.
2 lift - ed, where his pre - cious blood is spilled.
3 o - cean, by that flood from stain are freed.
4 i - ron! sweet - est weight is hung on thee.
5 beau - ty gent - ly on thine arms ex - tend.
6 glo - ry while e - ter - nal a - ges run.

Words: Venantius Honorius Fortunatus (540?-600?); ver. *Hymnal 1982*, after John Mason Neale (1818-1866)
Music: *Pange lingua*, plainsong, Mode 3, *Zisterzienser Hymnar*, 14th cent.   87. 87. 87

The Confession of Sin

The Deacon or Celebrant says

Let us confess our sins against God and our neighbor.

Silence may be kept.

Minister and People

Most merciful God,
we confess that we have sinned against you
in thought, word, and deed,
by what we have done,
and by what we have left undone.
We have not loved you with our whole heart;
we have not loved our neighbors as ourselves.
We are truly sorry and we humbly repent.
For the sake of your Son Jesus Christ,
have mercy on us and forgive us;
that we may delight in your will,
and walk in your ways,
to the glory of your Name. Amen.

The Priest, stands and says

Almighty God have mercy on you, forgive you all your
sins through our Lord Jesus Christ, strengthen you in all
goodness, and by the power of the Holy Spirit keep you in
eternal life. *Amen.*

The Lord's Prayer

Celebrant And now as our Savior Christ has taught us, we are bold to say,

Celebrant and People

Our Father, who art in heaven,
 hallowed be thy Name,
 thy kingdom come, thy will be done,
 on earth as it is in heaven.
Give us this day our daily bread.
And forgive us our trespasses,
 as we forgive those
 who trespass against us.
And lead us not into temptation,
 but deliver us from evil.
For thine is the kingdom and the power
 and the glory, forever and ever. *Amen.*

The Holy Communion

The Celebrant and Lay Eucharistic Ministers serve the Sacrament, pre-sanctified on Maundy Thursday.

During the distribution of the Body and Blood of Christ in this Holy Eucharist, the Hymn on page 130 is sung by the congregation.

A Hymn

"And Now O Father, Mindful of the Love"

1 And now, O Father, mindful of the love that
2 Look Father, look on his a-noint-ed face, and
*3 And then for those, our dear-est and our best, by
*4 And so we come; O draw us to thy feet, most

bought us, once for all, on Cal-vary's tree, and hav-ing with us
on-ly look on us as found in him; look not on our mis-
this pre-vail-ing pres-ence we ap-peal; O fold them clos-er
pa-tient Sa-vior, who canst love us still! And by this food, so

him that pleads a-bove, we here pre-sent, we here spread
us-ings of thy grace, our prayer so lan-guid, and our
to thy mer-cy's breast! O do thine ut-most for their
awe-some and so sweet, de-liv-er us from ev-ery

forth to thee, that on-ly of-fering per-fect in thine
faith so dim: for lo! be-tween our sins and their re-
soul's true weal! From taint-ing mis-chief keep them pure and
touch of ill: in thine own ser-vice make us glad and

eyes,	the	one	true,	pure,	im -	mor - tal	sac - ri -	fice.
ward,	we	set	the	pas - sion	of	thy Son	our	Lord.
clear,	and	crown thy	gifts with	strength	to	per - se -	vere.
free,	and	grant us	nev - er -	more	to	part from	thee.

Words: William Bright (1824-1901), alt.
Music: *Unde et memores*, William Henry Monk (1823-1889)

10 10. 10 10. 10 10

The Celebrant invites all to pray together

Lord Jesus Christ, Son of the living God, we pray you to
set your passion, cross, and death between your
judgment and our souls, now and in the hour of our
death. Give mercy and grace to the living; pardon and
rest to the dead; to your holy Church peace and concord;
and to us sinners everlasting life and glory; for with the
Father and the Holy Spirit you live and reign, one God,
now and for ever. *Amen.*

The congregation leaves in silent meditation.

The Liturgy of the Solemn Collects and the Stations of the Cross for Good Friday

All ministers enter the church dressed only in black cassock with no ornamentation, and take their places.

Celebrant As our Savior Christ in Gethsemane's Garden and again on Golgotha's Hill prayed for the world, let us too remember the creation and its creatures before the throne of God and the Lamb.

The Solemn Collects *All standing*

[Deacon or appointed Reader] Dear People of God: Our heavenly Father sent his Son into the world, not to condemn the world, but that the world through him might be saved; that all who believe in him might be delivered from the power of sin and death, and become heirs with him of everlasting life.

We pray, therefore, for people everywhere according to their needs. *The Celebrant and people kneel.*

The Celebrant prays the Collects.

Reader Let us pray for the holy Catholic Church of Christ throughout the world;

> For its unity in witness and service
> For all bishops and other ministers
> and the people whom they serve
> For *N.*, our Bishop, and all the people of this diocese
> For all Christians in this community
> For those about to be baptize (particularly_____)

That God will confirm his Church in faith, increase it in love, and preserve it in peace.

Silence

Celebrant   Almighty and everlasting God, by whose Spirit the whole body of your faithful people is governed and sanctified: Receive our supplications and prayers which we offer before you for all members of your holy Church, that in their vocation and ministry they may truly and devoutly serve you; through our Lord and Savior Jesus Christ. *Amen.*

Reader Let us pray for all nations and peoples of the earth, and for those in authority among them;

> For _____, the President of the United States
> For our Governor and State Legislature
> For the Congress and the Supreme Court
> For the Members and Representatives of the United Nations
> For all who are called on to serve the common good

That by God's help they may seek justice and truth, and live in peace and concord.

Silence

Almighty God, kindle, we pray, in every heart the true love of peace, and guide with your wisdom those who take counsel for the nations of the earth; that in tranquility your dominion may increase, until the earth is filled with the knowledge of your love; through Jesus Christ our Lord. *Amen.*

Reader Let us pray for all who suffer and are afflicted in body or in mind;
> For the hungry and the homeless, the destitute and the oppressed
> For the sick, the wounded, and the crippled

For those in loneliness, fear, and anguish
For those who face temptation, doubt, and despair
For the sorrowful and bereaved
For prisoners and captives, and those in mortal
danger

That God in his mercy will comfort and relieve them, and grant them the knowledge of his love, and stir up in us the will and patience to minister to their needs.

Silence

Celebrant Gracious God, the comfort of all who sorrow, the strength of all who suffer: Let the cry of those in misery and need come to you, that they may find your mercy present with them in all their afflictions; and give us, we pray, the strength to serve them for the sake of him who suffered for us, your Son Jesus Christ our Lord. *Amen.*

Reader Let us pray for all who have not received the Gospel of Christ;

For those who have never heard the word of salvation
For those who have lost their faith
For those hardened by sin or indifference
For the contemptuous and the scornful
For those who are enemies of the cross of Christ and
persecutors of his disciples
For those who in the name of Christ have persecuted others, that God will open their hearts to the truth, and lead them to faith and obedience.

Silence

Celebrant   Merciful God, creator of all the peoples of the earth and lover of souls: Have compassion on all who do not know you as you are revealed in your Son Jesus Christ; let your Gospel be preached with grace and power to those who have not heard it; turn the hearts of those who resist it; and bring home to your fold those who have gone astray; that there may be one flock under one shepherd, Jesus Christ our Lord.   *Amen.*

Reader   Let us commit ourselves to our God, and pray for the grace of a holy life, that, with all who have departed this world and have died in the peace of Christ, and those whose faith is known to God alone, we may be accounted worthy to enter into the fullness of the joy of our Lord, and receive the crown of life in the day of resurrection.

Silence

Celebrant   O God of unchangeable power and eternal light: Look favorably on your whole Church, that wonderful and sacred mystery; by the effectual working of your providence, carry out in tranquility the plan of salvation; let the whole world see and know that things which were cast down are being raised up, and things which had grown old are being made new, and that all things are being brought to their perfection by him through whom all things were made, your Son Jesus Christ our Lord; who lives and reigns with you, in the unity of the Holy Spirit, one God, for ever and ever. *Amen*

Anthem 1

Celebrant We glory in your cross, O Lord,

People *and praise and glorify your holy resurrection;*
for by virtue of your cross
joy has come to the whole world.

Celebrant May God be merciful to us and bless us,
show us the light of his countenance, and
come to us.

People *Let your ways be known upon earth,*
your saving health among all nations.

Celebrant Let the peoples praise you, O God;
let all the peoples praise you.

People *We glory in your cross, O Lord,*
and praise and glorify your holy resurrection;
for by virtue of your cross
joy has come to the whole world.

Anthem 2

Celebrant We adore you, O Christ, and we bless you,

People *because by your holy cross you have redeemed*
the world.

Celebrant If we have died with him, we shall also live
with him; if we endure, we shall also reign with him.

People *We adore you, O Christ, and we bless you,*
because by your holy cross you have redeemed the world.

Anthem 3

Celebrant O Savior of the world, who by your cross and precious blood you have redeemed us:

People *Save us and help us, we humbly beseech thee, O Lord.*

A Hymn

"Where He Leads Me, I Will Follow"

E. W. Blandy, 19th century   John H. Norris, 1844-1907

Opening Devotions

Officiant *In the Name of the Father, and of the Son, and of the Holy Spirit. Amen.*

Officiant   *Lord, have mercy.*
People   Christ, have mercy.
Officiant   *Lord, have mercy.*

Officiant and People

Our Father, who art in heaven,
hallowed by Thy name.
Thy kingdom come.
Thy will be done,
on earth as it is in heaven.
Give us this day our daily bread,
and forgive us our trespasses,
as we forgive those who trespass against us.
Lead us not into temptation,
but deliver us from evil.

Officiant   We will glory in the cross of our Lord Jesus
Christ; in whom is our salvation, our life and
resurrection. Let us pray. (Silence is kept)

Officiant   Assist us mercifully with your help, O Lord,
God of our salvation, that we may enter with joy upon the
contemplation of those mighty acts, whereby You have
given us life and immortality; through Jesus Christ our
Lord. Amen.

THE FIRST STATION
JESUS IS CONDEMNED TO DEATH

Officiant and People We adore You, O Christ, and we
bless You: because by Your holy cross You have
redeemed the world.

Lector As soon as it was morning, the chief priests, with the elders and scribes, and the whole council, held a consultation; and they bound Jesus and led Him away and delivered him to Pilate. And they all condemned Him and said, "He deserves to die." When Pilate heard these words, he brought Jesus out and sat down on the judgment seat at a place called the Pavement, but in the Hebrew, Gabbatha. Then he handed Jesus over to them to be crucified.

Officiant God did not spare His own Son:
             But delivered Him up for us all.

Let us pray. (Silence)

Almighty God, whose most dear Son went not up to joy but first He suffered pain, and entered not into glory before He was crucified: Mercifully grant that we, walking in the way of the cross, may find it none other than the way of life and peace; through Jesus Christ Your Son our Lord. Amen.

The Trisagion [repeated three times by *Officiant & People*]

Holy God,
Holy and Mighty,
Holy Immortal One,
Have mercy upon us.

(All sing)
Where He leads me I will follow,
Where He leads me I will follow,
Where He leads me I will follow,
I'll go with Him, with Him all the way.

SECOND STATION
JESUS TAKES UP HIS CROSS

Officiant and People We adore You, O Christ, and we
bless You: Because by Your holy cross You have
redeemed the world.

Jesus went out, bearing His own cross, to the place
called the place of the skull, which is called in Hebrew,
Golgotha. Although He was a son, He learned obedience
through what He suffered. Like a lamb He was led to the
slaughter; and like a sheep that before its shearers is
mute, so He opened not His mouth. Worthy is the Lamb
who was slain, to receive power and riches and wisdom
and strength and honor and glory and blessing.

The Lord has laid on Him the iniquity of us all:
For the transgression of my people was He stricken.

Let us pray. (Silence)

Almighty God, whose beloved Son willingly endured the
agony and shame of the cross for our redemption: Give
us courage to take up our cross and follow Him; who
lives and reigns for ever and ever. Amen.

Holy God,
Holy and Mighty,
Holy Immortal One,
Have mercy upon us.

(All sing)

Where He leads me I will follow,
Where He leads me I will follow,
Where He leads me I will follow,
I'll go with Him, with Him all the way.

THIRD STATION
JESUS FALLS THE FIRST TIME

Officiant and People We adore You, O Christ, and we bless You: Because by Your holy cross You have redeemed the world.

Christ Jesus, though He was in the form of God, did not count equality with God a thing to be grasped; but emptied Himself, taking the form of a servant, and was born in human likeness. And being found in human form He humbled Himself and became obedient unto death, even death on a cross. Therefore God has highly exalted Him, and bestowed on Him the name which is above every name. Come, let us bow down, and bend the knee, and kneel before the Lord our maker, for He is the Lord our God.

Surely He has borne our griefs:
And carried our sorrows.

Let us pray. (Silence)

O God, you know us to be set in the midst of so many and great dangers, that by reason of the frailty of our nature we cannot always stand upright: Grant us such strength and protection as may support us in all dangers, and carry us through all temptation; through Jesus Christ our Lord. Amen.

Holy God,
Holy and Mighty,
Holy Immortal One,
Have mercy upon us.

(All sing)

Where He leads me I will follow,
Where He leads me I will follow,
Where He leads me I will follow,
I'll go with Him, with Him all the way.

FOURTH STATION
THE CROSS IS LAID ON SIMON OF CYRENE

Officiant and People We adore You, O Christ, and we bless You: Because by Your holy cross You have redeemed the world.

As they led Jesus away, they came upon a man of Cyrene, Simon by name, who was coming in from the country, and laid on him the cross to carry it behind Jesus. "If anyone would come after me, let him deny himself and take up his cross and follow me. Take my yoke upon you, and learn from me; for my yoke is easy, and my burden is light."

Whoever does not bear his own cross and come after me, Cannot be my disciple.

Let us pray. (Silence)

Heavenly Father, whose blessed Son came not to be served but to serve: Bless all who, following in His steps, give themselves to the service of others; that with wisdom, patience, and courage, they may minister in His Name to the suffering, the friendless, and the needy, for the love of Him who laid down His life for us, Your Son our Savior Jesus Christ. Amen.

Holy God,
Holy and Mighty,
Holy Immortal One,
Have mercy upon us.

(All sing)

Where He leads me I will follow,
Where He leads me I will follow,
Where He leads me I will follow,
I'll go with Him, with Him all the way.

FIFTH STATION
JESUS FALLS A SECOND TIME

Officiant and People We adore You, O Christ, and we
bless You: Because by Your holy cross You have
redeemed the world.

Surely He has borne our griefs and carried our sorrows.
All we like sheep have gone astry; we have turned every
one to his own way; and the Lord has laid on Him the
iniquity of us all. He was oppressed, and He was
afflicted, yet He opened not His mouth. For the
transgression of my people was He stricken.

But as for me, I am a worm and no man.
Scorned by all and despised by the people.

Let us pray. (Silence)

Almighty and everliving God, in Your tender love for the
human race You sent Your Son our Savior Jesus Christ
to take upon Him our nature, and to suffer death upon
the cross, giving us the example of His great humility.

Mercifully grant that we may walk in the way of His suffering, and also share in His resurrection; who lives and reigns for ever and ever. Amen.

Holy God,
Holy and Mighty,
Holy Immortal One,
Have mercy upon us.

(All sing)

Where He leads me I will follow,
Where He leads me I will follow,
Where He leads me I will follow,
I'll go with Him, with Him all the way.

SIXTH STATION
JESUS MEETS THE WOMEN OF JERUSALEM

Officiant & People We adore You, O Christ, and we bless You: Because by Your holy cross You have redeemed the world.

There followed after Jesus a great multitude of the people, and among them were some women who bewailed and lamented Him. But Jesus, turning to them, said "Daughters of Jerusalem, do not weep for me, but weep for yourselves and for your children."

Those who sowed with tears,
Will reap with songs of joy.

Let us pray, (Silence)

Teach Your Church, O Lord, to mourn the sins of which it is guilty, and to repent and forsake them; that by Your pardoning grace, the results of our iniquities may not be visited upon our children and our children's children, through Jesus Christ our Lord. Amen.

Holy God,
Holy and Mighty,
Holy Immortal One,
Have mercy upon us.

(All sing)

Where He leads me I will follow,
Where He leads me I will follow,
Where He leads me I will follow,
I'll go with Him, with Him all the way.

SEVENTH STATION
JESUS IS STRIPPED OF HIS GARMENTS

Officiant and People We adore You, O Christ, and we bless You: Because by Your holy cross You have redeemed the world.

When they came to a place called Golgotha (which means the place of the skull), they offered Him wine to drink, mingled with gall; but when He tasted it, He would not drink it. And they divided His garments among them by casting lots. This was to fulfill the scripture which says, "They divided my garments among them; they cast lots for my clothing."

They gave me gall to eat:
And when I was thirsty they gave me vinegar to drink.

Let us pray. (Silence)

Lord God, whose blessed Son our Savior gave His body to be whipped and His face to be spit upon: Give us grace to accept joyfully the sufferings of the present time, confident of the glory that shall be revealed, through Jesus Christ our Lord. Amen.

Holy God,
Holy and Mighty,
Holy Immortal One,
Have mercy upon us.

(All sing)

Where He leads me I will follow,
Where He leads me I will follow,
Where He leads me I will follow,
I'll go with Him, with Him all the way.

EIGHTH STATION
JESUS IS NAILED TO THE CROSS

Officiant and People We adore You, O Christ, and we bless You: Because by Your holy cross You have redeemed the world.

When they came to the place which is called The Skull, there they crucified Him; and with Him they crucified two criminals, one on the right, the other on the left, and Jesus between them. And scripture was fulfilled which says, "He was numbered with the transgressors."

They pierce my hands and my feet.
They stare and gloat over me.

(All sing)

Were you there
when they nailed Him to the cross?
Were you there when they nailed Him to the cross?
Oh, sometimes it causes me to tremble, tremble, tremble.
Were you there when they nailed Him to the cross?

Let us pray. (Silence)

Lord Jesus Christ, You stretched out Your arms of love
on the hard wood of the cross that everyone might come
within the reach of Your saving embrace: So clothe us in
Your Spirit that we, reaching forth our hands in love,
may bring those who do not know You the knowledge and
love of You; for the honor of Your Name. Amen.

Holy God,
Holy and Mighty,
Holy Immortal One,
Have mercy upon us.

(All sing)

Where He leads me I will follow,
Where He leads me I will follow,
Where He leads me I will follow,
I'll go with Him, with Him all the way.

NINTH STATION
JESUS DIES ON THE CROSS

Officiant and People We adore You, O Christ, and we bless You: Because by Your holy cross You have redeemed the world.

When Jesus saw His mother, and the disciple whom He loved standing near, He said to His mother, "Woman, behold your son!" Then He said to the disciple, "Behold your mother!" and when Jesus had received the vinegar, He said, "It is finished!" And then, crying with a loud voice, He said, "Father, into your hands I commend my spirit." And He bowed His head, and handed over His spirit.

Christ for us became obedient unto death,
Even death on a cross.

Let us pray. (Silence)

Our God, who for our redemption gave Your only begotten Son to the death of the cross, and by His glorious resurrection delivered us from the power of our enemy: Grant us so to die daily to sin, that we may evermore live with Him in the joy of His resurrection; who lives and reigns now and for ever. Amen.

Holy God,
Holy and Mighty,
Holy Immortal One,
Have mercy upon us.

(All sing)

Where He leads me I will follow,
Where He leads me I will follow,
Where He leads me I will follow,
I'll go with Him, with Him all the way.

TENTH STATION
JESUS IS LAID IN THE TOMB

Officiant and People We adore You, O Christ, and we
bless You: Because by Your holy cross You have
redeemed the world.

When it was evening, there came a rich man from
Arimathea, named Joseph, who also was disciple of
Jesus. He went to Pilate and asked for the body of Jesus.
The Pilate ordered it to be given to him. And Joseph took
the body, and wrapped it in a clean linen shroud, and
laid it in his own new tomb, which he had hewn in the
rock; and he rolled a great stone to the door of the tomb.

You will not abandon me to the grave,
Nor let Your Holy One see corruption.

(All sing)

Were you there when they laid Him in the tomb?
Were you there when they laid Him in the tomb?
Oh, sometimes it causes me to tremble, tremble, tremble.
Were you there when they laid Him in the tomb?

Let us pray. (Silence)

O God, Your blessed Son was laid in a tomb in a garden, and rested on the Sabbath day; Grant that we who have been buried with Him in the waters of baptism may find our perfect rest in his eternal and glorious kingdom; where He lives and reigns for ever and ever. Amen.

Holy God,
Holy and Mighty,
Holy Immortal One,
Have mercy upon us.

(All sing)

Where He leads me I will follow,
Where He leads me I will follow,
Where He leads me I will follow,
I'll go with Him, with Him all the way.

CONCLUDING PRAYERS BEFORE THE ALTAR

Officiant   Savior of the world, by Your cross and precious blood You have redeemed us:

People   Save us, and help us, we humbly beseech You, O Lord.

Officiant   Let us pray. (Silence)

We thank You, heavenly Father, that You have delivered us from the dominion of sin and death and brought us into the kingdom of Your Son; and we pray that, as by His death He has recalled us to life, so by His love He may raise us to the eternal joys; who lives and reigns with You, in the unity of the Holy Spirit, one God, now and for ever. Amen.

The congregation departs in silence.

The Great Vigil

of

Easter

The Lighting of the Paschal Candle

> *In the darkness, fire is kindled at a distance from the church [with seating for those who need it After this the Celebrant addresses the people with these words*

Celebrant Dear friends in Christ: On this most holy night, in which our Lord Jesus passed over from death to life, the Church invites her members, dispersed throughout the world, to gather in vigil and prayer. For this is the Passover of the Lord, in which, by hearing his Word and celebrating his Sacraments, we share in his victory over death.

Let us pray.

O God, through your Son you have bestowed upon your people the brightness of your light: Sanctify this new fire, and grant that in this Paschal feast we may so burn with heavenly desires, that with pure minds we may attain to the festival of everlasting light; through Jesus Christ our Lord. *Amen.*

The Paschal Candle is then lighted from the newly kindled fire, and leads the procession toward the chancel, pausing three times and singing

Celebrant The light of Christ.
People Thanks be to God.

The Paschal Candle is placed in its stand.

The Exultet – *Read or sung by Deacon [music is found in the Altar missal]*

Rejoice now, heavenly hosts and choirs of angels,
and let your trumpets shout Salvation
for the victory of our mighty King.

Rejoice and sing now, all the round earth,
bright with a glorious splendor,
for darkness has been vanquished by our eternal King.

Rejoice and be glad now, Mother Church,
and let your holy courts, in radiant light,
resound with the praises of your people.

All you who stand near this marvelous and holy flame,
pray with me to God the Almighty
for the grace to sing the worthy praise of this great light;
through Jesus Christ his Son our Lord,
who lives and reigns with him,
in the unity of the Holy Spirit,
one God, for ever and ever. *Amen.*

Deacon The Lord be with you.
Answer And also with you.
Deacon Let us give thanks to the Lord our God.
Answer It is right to give him thanks and praise.
Deacon It is truly right and good, always and everywhere, with our whole heart and mind and voice, to praise you, the invisible, almighty, and eternal God, and your only-begotten Son, Jesus Christ our Lord; for he is

the true Paschal Lamb, who at the feast of the Passover paid for us the debt of Adam's sin, and by his blood delivered your faithful people.

This is the night, when you brought our fathers, the children of Israel, out of bondage in Egypt, and led them through the Red Sea on dry land.

This is the night, when all who believe in Christ are delivered from the gloom of sin, and are restored to grace and holiness of life.

This is the night, when Christ broke the bonds of death and hell, and rose victorious from the grave.

How wonderful and beyond our knowing, O God, is your mercy and loving-kindness to us, that to redeem a slave, you gave a Son.

How holy is this night, when wickedness is put to flight, and sin is washed away. It restores innocence to the fallen, and joy to those who mourn. It casts out pride and hatred, and brings peace and concord.

How blessed is this night, when earth and heaven are joined and man is reconciled to God.

Holy Father, accept our evening sacrifice, the offering of this candle in your honor. May it shine continually to drive away all darkness. May Christ, the Morning Star who knows no setting, find it ever burning—he who gives his light to all creation, and who lives and reigns for ever and ever. *Amen.*

The Liturgy of the Word

Let us hear the record of God's saving deeds in history, how he saved his people in ages past; and let us pray that our God will bring each of us to the fullness of redemption.

Israel's deliverance at the Red Sea
Exodus 14:10-15:1

As Pharaoh drew near, the Israelites looked back, and there were the Egyptians advancing on them. In great fear the Israelites cried out to the LORD. They said to Moses, "Was it because there were no graves in Egypt that you have taken us away to die in the wilderness? What have you done to us, bringing us out of Egypt? Is this not the very thing we told you in Egypt, 'Let us alone and let us serve the Egyptians'? For it would have been better for us to serve the Egyptians than to die in the wilderness." But Moses said to the people, "Do not be afraid, stand firm, and see the deliverance that the LORD will accomplish for you today; for the Egyptians whom you see today you shall never see again. The LORD will fight for you, and you have only to keep still."

Then the LORD said to Moses, "Why do you cry out to me? Tell the Israelites to go forward. But you lift up your staff, and stretch out your hand over the sea and divide it, that the Israelites may go into the sea on dry ground. Then I will harden the hearts of the Egyptians so that they will go in after them; and so I will gain glory for myself over Pharaoh and all his army, his chariots, and his chariot drivers. And the Egyptians shall know that I am the LORD, when I have gained glory for myself over Pharaoh, his chariots, and his chariot drivers."

The angel of God who was going before the Israelite army moved and went behind them; and the pillar of cloud moved from in front of them and took its place behind them. It came between the army of Egypt and the army of Israel. And so the cloud was there with the darkness, and it lit up the night; one did not come near the other all night.

Then Moses stretched out his hand over the sea. The LORD drove the sea back by a strong east wind all night, and turned the sea into dry land; and the waters were divided. The Israelites went into the sea on dry ground, the waters forming a wall for them on their right and on their left. The Egyptians pursued, and went into the sea after them, all of Pharaoh's horses, chariots, and chariot drivers. At the morning watch the LORD in the pillar of fire and cloud looked down upon the Egyptian army, and threw the Egyptian army into panic. He clogged their chariot wheels so that they turned with difficulty. The Egyptians said, "Let us flee from the Israelites, for the LORD is fighting for them against Egypt."

Then the LORD said to Moses, "Stretch out your hand over the sea, so that the water may come back upon the Egyptians, upon their chariots and chariot drivers." So Moses stretched out his hand over the sea, and at dawn the sea returned to its normal depth. As the Egyptians fled before it, the LORD tossed the Egyptians into the sea. The waters returned and covered the chariots and the chariot drivers, the entire army of Pharaoh that had followed them into the sea; not one of them remained. But the Israelites walked on dry ground through the sea, the waters forming a wall for them on their right and on their left.

Thus the LORD saved Israel that day from the Egyptians; and Israel saw the Egyptians dead on the seashore. Israel saw the great work that the LORD did against the Egyptians. So the people feared the LORD and believed in the LORD and in his servant Moses.

Then the prophet Miriam, Aaron's sister, took a tambourine in her hand; and all the women went out after her with tambourines and with dancing. And Miriam sang to them:

"Sing to the LORD, for he has triumphed gloriously; horse and rider he has thrown into the sea."

Canticle 8   BCP, page 85

Canticle 8 "The Horse and Rider"

Let us pray.   *(Silence)*

O God, whose wonderful deeds of old shine forth even to our own day, you once delivered by the power of your mighty arm your chosen people from slavery under Pharaoh, to be a sign for us of the salvation of all nations by the water of Baptism: Grant that all the peoples of the earth may be numbered among the offspring of Abraham, and rejoice in the inheritance of Israel; through Jesus Christ our Lord. *Amen.*

God's Presence in a renewed Israel
Isaiah [4:2-6]
Psalm [122], BCP page 779

Let us pray.   *(Silence)*

O God, you led your ancient people by a pillar of cloud by day and a pillar of fire by night: Grant that we, who serve you now on earth, may come to the joy of that heavenly Jerusalem, where all tears are wiped away and where your saints for ever sing your praise; through Jesus Christ our Lord. *Amen.*

Salvation offered freely to all

Isaiah [55:1-11]

Psalm [42] BCP, page 643

As The Deer Longs for Water

Michael Baughen

Michael Baughen
arr David Wilson
7 6 10 6

1. As the deer longs for wa-ter My soul longs for
2. In the past I was lead-ing The praise in your
3. Thru the day He shows mer-cy, And so, in the

you, Lord, My soul is thir-sty for the liv-ing God—
house, Lord, With shouts of thank-ful joy a-midst the crowd—
e-v'ning, I sing to Him with praise up-on my lips—

I long to see His face. Day and night I am weep-ing, My
Yet now I am de-pressed. Why, my soul, are you down-cast? And
In my life He is God. Why, my soul, are you down-cast? And

soul is poured out, Lord, Each day I hear it said, "Where
why are you groan-ing? Re-new your hope in God, and
why are you groan-ing? Re-new your hope in God, and

is your God?" I long to see your face.
praise Him still— He is your sav-ing help.
praise Him still— He is your sav-ing help.

Let us pray.   *(Silence)*

O God, you have created all things by the power of your Word, and you renew the earth by your Spirit: Give now the water of life to those who thirst for you, that they may bring forth abundant fruit in your glorious kingdom; through Jesus Christ our Lord. *Amen.*

O God of unchangeable power and eternal light: Look favorably on your whole Church, that wonderful and sacred mystery; by the effectual working of your providence, carry out in tranquility the plan of salvation; let the whole world see and know that things which were cast down are being raised up, and things which had grown old are being made new, and that all things are being brought to their perfection by him through whom all things were made, your Son Jesus Christ our Lord. *Amen.*

A homily may be preached after any of the preceding Readings.

Holy Baptism (beginning with the Presentation of the Candidates, page 301, and concluding with the reception of the newly baptized) may be administered here. In the absence of candidates for Baptism or Confirmation, the Celebrant leads the people in the Renewal of Baptismal Vows.

Celebrant [all standing]

Through the Paschal mystery, dear friends, we are buried with Christ by Baptism into his death, and raised with him to newness of life. I call upon you, therefore, now that our Lenten observance is ended, to renew the solemn promises and vows of Holy Baptism, by which we once renounced Satan and all his works, and promised to serve God faithfully in his holy Catholic Church.

The Renewal of Baptismal Vows

Celebrant Do you reaffirm your renunciation of evil and
        renew your commitment to Jesus Christ?
People   I do.

Celebrant Do you believe in God the Father?
People   I believe in God, the Father almighty,
        creator of heaven and earth.
Celebrant   Do you believe in Jesus Christ, the Son of
        God?
People   I believe in Jesus Christ, his only Son, our Lord.
        He was conceived by the power of the Holy
        Spirit and born of the Virgin Mary.
        He suffered under Pontius Pilate,
          was crucified, died, and was buried.
        He descended to the dead.
        On the third day he rose again.
        He ascended into heaven,
          and is seated at the right hand of the Father.
        He will come again to judge the living and the
        dead.

Celebrant Do you believe in God the Holy Spirit?
People I believe in the Holy Spirit,
        the holy catholic Church,
        the communion of saints,
        the forgiveness of sins,
        the resurrection of the body,
        and the life everlasting.

Celebrant Will you continue in the apostles' teaching and
        fellowship, in the breaking of bread, and in the
        prayers?
People I will, with God's help.

Celebrant Will you persevere in resisting evil, and, whenever you fall into sin, repent and return to the Lord?

People I will, with God's help.

Celebrant Will you proclaim by word and example the Good News of God in Christ?

People I will, with God's help.

Celebrant Will you seek and serve Christ in all persons, loving your neighbor as yourself?

People I will, with God's help.

Celebrant Will you strive for justice and peace among all people, and respect the dignity of every human being?

People I will, with God's help.

The Celebrant concludes the Renewal of Vows as follows

May Almighty God, the Father of our Lord Jesus Christ, who has given us a new birth by water and the Holy Spirit, and bestowed upon us the forgiveness of sins, keep us in eternal life by his grace, in Christ Jesus our Lord. *Amen.*

O God of unchangeable power and eternal light: Look favorably on your whole Church, that wonderful and sacred mystery; by the effectual working of your providence, carry out in tranquility the plan of salvation; let the whole world see and know that things which were cast down are being raised up, and things which had grown old are being made new, and that all things are being brought to their perfection by him through whom all things were made, your Son Jesus Christ our Lord. *Amen.*

The Congregation Sings *"Darkness is Gone!"*

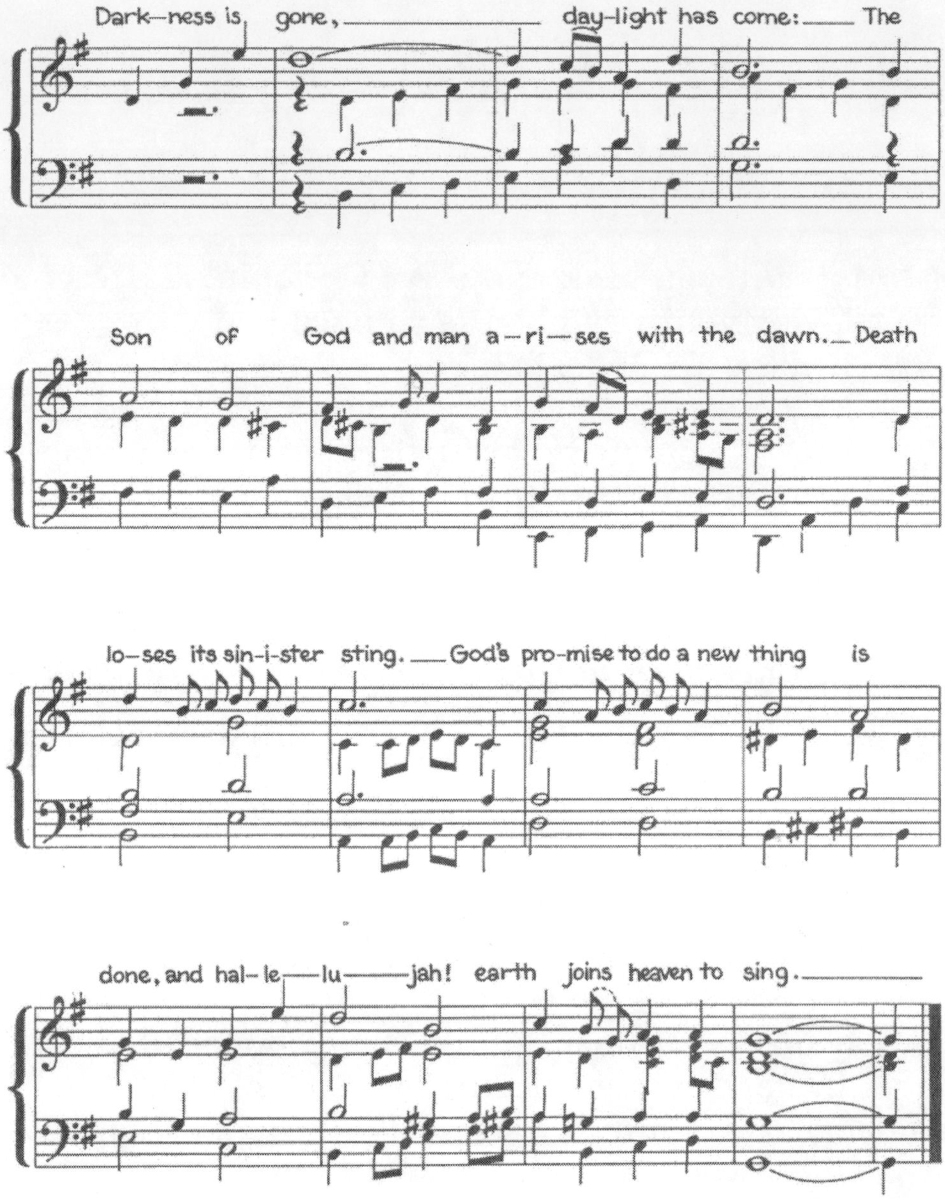

1. Darkness is gone, daylight has come:
   The Son of God and man arises with the dawn.
   Death loses its sinister sting:
   God's promise to do a new thing
   Is done, and Hallelujah!
   Earth joins heaven to sing.

2. See now the cross, see now the grave:
   They, vacant, celebrate how God's foolishness can save.
   The criminal nailed up as a fraud
   Is raised by the power of God
   And lives. So, Hallelujah!
   Scatter the news abroad.

3. Greener the grass, brighter the sun,
   The God-loved world proclaims a new age has begun.
   Creation is decked for her guest
   Who, freed from his grave clothes is dressed
   In light and, Hallelujah!
   Tells that the earth is blessed.

4. The needed trust, the longed-for peace
   Are passed as hands from sword and shackle are released.
   The violence of hate reigns no more:
   The victory of love is the core
   Of hope and, Hallelujah!
   Love means an open door.

5. "The Kingdom comes!" the King proclaims:
   Justice and joy abound where Christ-filled faith pertains.
   Religion, remote and typecast,
   Is gone and the future is vast.
   New tongues sing, "Hallelujah!
    God is for us at last!"

6. Enrol the drum, enlist the gong
   To celebrate in sound that right has conquered wrong.
   Join hands with the neighbour unknown,
   Unite through the love that is shown
   In Christ, for, Hallelujah!
   He is our Lord alone.

Only sing all six verses when the song is being used as a recessional —
which was its original intention. To shorten it, stop at verse 5, or omit
verses 4 and 5.

The First Eucharist of the Resurrection

The candles at the Altar may now be lighted from the Paschal Candle.

Celebrant   Alleluia. Christ is risen.
People   The Lord is risen indeed. Alleluia.

One of the following Canticles is then sung

Gloria in excelsis
Te Deum laudamus
Pascha nostrum

The Celebrant   The Lord be with you.
People   And also with you.
Celebrant   Let us pray.

The Celebrant says one of the following Collects

Almighty God, who for our redemption gave your only-begotten Son to the death of the cross, and by his glorious resurrection delivered us from the power of our enemy: Grant us so to die daily to sin, that we may evermore live with him in the joy of his resurrection; through Jesus Christ your Son our Lord, who lives and reigns with you and the Holy Spirit, one God, now and for ever. *Amen.*

or this

O God, who made this most holy night to shine with the glory of the Lord's resurrection: Stir up in your Church that Spirit of adoption which is given to us in Baptism, that we, being renewed both in body and mind, may worship you in sincerity and truth; through Jesus Christ our Lord, who lives and reigns with you, in the unity of the Holy Spirit, one God, now and for ever. *Amen.*

The Epistle Romans [6:3-11]

The Sequence Hymn   *"One Day!"*

CHAPMAN 11.10.11.10. with Refrain
Charles H. Marsh, 1886-1956

J. Wilbur Chapman, 1859-1918

1. One day when heav - en was filled with His prais - es, One day when
2. One day they led Him up Cal - va - ry's moun - tain, One day they
3. One day they left Him a - lone in the gar - den, One day He
4. One day the grave could con - ceal Him no long - er, One day the
5. One day the trum - pet will sound for His com - ing, One day the

sin was as black as could be, Je - sus came forth to be
nailed Him to die on the tree; Suf - fer - ing an - guish, de -
rest - ed, from suf - fer - ing free; An - gels came down o'er His
stone rolled a - way from the door; Then He a - rose, o - ver
skies with His glo - ry will shine; Won - der - ful day, my be -

born of a Vir - gin, Dwelt a - mong men, my ex - am - ple is He!
spised and re - ject - ed, Bear - ing our sins, my Re - deem - er is He!
tomb to keep vig - il; Hope of the hope - less, my Sav - iour is He!
death He has con - quered; Now is as - cend - ed, my Lord ev - er - more!
lov - ed ones bring - ing; Glo - ri - ous Sav - iour, this Je - sus is mine!

REFRAIN

Liv - ing, He loved me; dy - ing, He saved me; Bur - ied, He

172

car - ried my sins far a - way; Ris - ing, He jus - ti - fied

free - ly for - ev - er: One day He's com - ing— oh, glo - ri - ous day!

The Holy Gospel of our Lord Jesus Christ According to
Matthew [28:1-10]

The Sermon

The Nicene Creed is not used at this service.

Holy Baptism, Confirmation, or the Renewal of Baptismal Vows may take place here.

The celebration continues with the Prayers of the People.

Intercessor Living Christ, you are risen from the dead! Love reigns! You are life stronger than death. Raise our eyes to see you as the new day dawns.

We pray for the Church. Today we offer our joy that we celebrate your glorious resurrection with our brothers and sisters around the world. Envelop your people with a sense of your risen presence, today and always. (the people may add their prayers, spoken or unspoken)

For the household of faith, the church of the risen Christ, we pray:

People   Be with us and bless us, O God.

Intercessor We pray for our nation. God of hope, teach us the difference between reaching down and reaching out. Guide the many of privilege who determine the destinies of others. Lead us not only to share our wealth, but to enter with hope into the poverty of those who do not share our good fortune. (Personal petitions are invited).

For our nation and for our common good, we pray:

People   Be with us and guide us, O God.

Intercessor We pray for the whole world. God of creation you have given us a world of glorious diversity. Give us the eyes to see the beauty of your cosmic patchwork. Give us open hearts and the confidence to invite all into the bond of your love, that in unity with you, we may bring your peace and goodness and vision to all people. (All are invited to add prayers).
For the welfare of our world, we pray:

People   Be with us and unite us, O God.

Intercessor We pray for this community. God who came to earth as one of us, help us see you in each member of this community. Bless the many gifts of our members and keep before us the image of the Servant Jesus, that joined with him we remain ready to kneel with basin and towel before each other and before those you continue to bring into our midst. (All are invited to add additional prayers) For our community we pray:

People Be with us and help us, O God.

We pray for all who suffer. God of compassion, open our hearts to bind and heal in your name. Bless all of those who ask our prayers, and give us courage to learn the names of others. Be present, through us, to those who need your comfort. (the people may add their prayers, spoken or unspoken)
For all who suffer and struggle, we pray:

People Be with us and heal us, O God.

We pray for all who have died. God who has loved us from before birth and God who loves us beyond the grave, we remember those who have died in the glorious hope of the resurrection, and we remember those who mourn, that they may be assured with that same hope. (the people may add their prayers, spoken or unspoken)
For all who have entered new life in Christ's resurrection, we pray:

People Be with us and raise us, 0 God.

Celebrant Glorious Lord of Life, we praise you, that by the wondrous resurrection of your Son, you have delivered us from sin and death and made your whole creation new; grant that we who celebrate with joy Christ's rising from the dead, may be raised from the death of sin to the life of righteousness; through him who lives and reigns with you and the Holy Spirit, one God now and for ever. *Amen.*

--Susanne Watson Epting, used by permission

The Peace

Celebrant The peace of the Lord be always with you.
People And also with you.

The Offertory [An appropriate hymn or chorus of resurrection life may be sung]

The Doxology *all stand*

Praise God from whom all blessings flow;
Praise him all creatures here, below.
Praise him above, ye heavenly hosts.
Praise Father, Son, and Holy Ghost. Amen.

The people remain standing.

The Sursum Corda

Celebrant   The Lord be with you.
People   And also with you.
Celebrant   Lift up your hearts.
People   We lift them to the Lord.
Celebrant   Let us give thanks to the Lord our God.
People   It is right to give him thanks and praise.

Celebrant It is right, and a good and joyful thing, always and everywhere to give thanks to you, Father Almighty, Creator of heaven and earth through Jesus Christ our Lord. But chiefly are we bound to praise you for the glorious resurrection of your Son Jesus Christ our Lord; for he is the true Paschal Lamb, who was sacrificed for us, and has taken away the sin of the world. By his death he has destroyed death, and by his rising to life again he has won for us everlasting life. Therefore we praise you, joining our voices with Angels and Archangels and with

all the company of heaven, who for ever sing this Hymn
to proclaim the glory of your Name:

Celebrant and People

Holy, holy, holy Lord, God of power and might,
heaven and earth are full of your glory.
  Hosanna in the highest.
Blessed is he who comes in the name of the Lord.
  Hosanna in the highest.

The people stand or kneel.

Celebrant

We give thanks to you, O God, for the goodness and love
which you have made known to us in creation; in the
calling of Israel to be your people; in your Word spoken
through the prophets; and above all in the Word made
flesh, Jesus, your Son. For in these last days you sent
him to be incarnate from the Virgin Mary, to be the
Savior and Redeemer of the world. In him, you have
delivered us from evil, and made us worthy to stand
before you. In him, you have brought us out of error
into truth, out of sin into righteousness, out of death into
life.

On the night before he died for us, our Lord Jesus Christ
took bread; and when he had given thanks to you, he
broke it, and gave it to his disciples, and said, "Take, eat:
This is my Body, which is given for you. Do this for the
remembrance of me."

After supper he took the cup of wine; and when he had
given thanks, he gave it to them, and said, "Drink this,
all of you: This is my Blood of the new Covenant, which is

shed for you and for many for the forgiveness of sins. Whenever you drink it, do this for the remembrance of me."

Therefore, according to his command, O Father,

Celebrant and People

We remember his death,
We proclaim his resurrection,
We await his coming in glory;

Celebrant   And we offer our sacrifice of praise and thanksgiving to you, O Lord of all; presenting to you, from your creation, this bread and this wine.

We pray you, gracious God, to send your Holy Spirit upon these gifts that they may be the Sacrament of the Body of Christ and his Blood of the new Covenant. Unite us to your Son in his sacrifice, that we may be acceptable through him, being sanctified by the Holy Spirit. In the fullness of time, put all things in subjection under your Christ, and bring us to that heavenly country where, with the Blessed Virgin Mary, St. Joseph, [_____. and] all your Saints, we may enter the everlasting heritage of your sons and daughters; through Jesus Christ our Lord, the firstborn of all creation, the head of the Church, and the author of our salvation.

By him, and with him, and in him, in the unity of the Holy Spirit all honor and glory is yours, Almighty Father, now and for ever. *AMEN.*

The Lord's Prayer

Celebrant   And now as our Savior Christ has taught us, we are bold to say,
Celebrant and People Our Father, who art in heaven,
 hallowed be thy Name,
 thy kingdom come, thy will be done,
 on earth as it is in heaven.
Give us this day our daily bread.
And forgive us our trespasses,
 as we forgive those who trespass against us.
And lead us not into temptation, but deliver us from evil.
For thine is the kingdom and the power
 and the glory, forever and ever.   *Amen.*

The Holy Communion

Celebrant Christ our Passover is sacrificed for us.
People Therefore let us keep the feast.
Celebrant The gifts of God for the people of God. Take them in remembrance that Christ died for you, and feed on him in your hearts by faith.

The Postcommunion Prayer

Celebrant Let us pray.
Celebrant and People Almighty and everliving God, we thank you for feeding us with the spiritual food of the most precious Body and Blood of your Son our Savior Jesus Christ; and for assuring us in these holy mysteries that we are living members of the Body of your Son, and heirs of your eternal kingdom. And now, Father, send us out to do the work you have given us to do, to love and serve you as faithful witnesses of Christ our Lord. To him, to you, and to the Holy Spirit, be honor and glory, now and for ever. *Amen.*

The Priestly Blessing

The Processional Hymn

"I Know that my Redeemer Liveth"

MESSIAH C.M.

Charles Wesley, 1707-1788   Arrangement from *The Messiah*, George Frederick Handel, 1685-1759

1. I know that my Re - deem - er lives And ev - er prays for me;
2. I find Him lift - ing up my head; He brings sal - va - tion near;
3. He wills that I should ho - ly be: What can with - stand His will?
4. Je - sus, I hang up - on Thy Word: I stead - fast - ly be - lieve

A to - ken of His love He gives, A pledge of lib - er - ty.
His pres - ence makes me free in - deed, And He will soon ap - pear.
The coun - sel of His grace in me He sure - ly shall ful - fill.
Thou wilt re - turn and claim me, Lord, And to Thy - self re - ceive.

The Dismissal *People respond* Thanks be to God.
Alleluia. Alleluia.

The Holy Eucharist

According to the

Dominican Tradition

[PARTICULARLY APPROPRIATE TO HOLY WEEK CELEBRATIONS – THIS IS
ONE FORM USED BY THE SANTA ROSA HOUSE OF THE ORDER OF
PREACHERS – ANGLICAN, A HOUSE OF THE ANGLICAN DOMINICANS]

The Preparation

The People stand as the Priest and Server enter and genuflect before the Altar. The Priest unfolds the corporal and uncovers the chalice and prepares it at the Epistle side, pouring in a few drops of blessed water, and then he re-covers it on the corporal.

Priest Precede our actions with your inspiration, we beseech you, O Lord, and accompany them with your help, that all of our works may always begin from you, and having begun, may be finished through you; through Christ our Lord. *Amen.*

Standing before the center of the Altar, the Priest bows solemnly, and making the sign of the cross, says

In the Name of the Father and of the Son and of the Holy Spirit. *Amen.*

Priest Give praise to the Lord for he is good.
People His mercy endures forever.

[All kneel] *Silence is kept while the Priest and People prepare themselves for worship.*

The Confession

Priest Our help is in the Name of the Lord.
People Who made heaven and earth.
Priest [bowing before the center of the Altar] says
Remove from us, O Lord, all of our iniquities, that we may deserve to enter the Holy of Holies; through Christ our Lord. *Amen.*

The Priest then makes the sign of the Cross on the Altar and kisses it, and signing himself, goes to the Epistle side and recites the Introit.

The Introit

After reciting the Introit, the Priest remains at the Epistle side and begins the Kyrie.

Celebrant   Lord have mercy upon us.
People Christ have mercy upon us.
Celebrant   Lord have mercy upon us.

The Collect of the Day

Celebrant   The Lord be with you.
People And also with you.
Celebrant Let us pray.

The Celebrant prays the Collect

People Amen.

The Holy Scriptures

The Epistle [Congregation is seated]

Lector A Reading from_____.

Lector   The Word of the Lord.
People   Thanks be to God.

A Sequence Hymn appropriate to the day may be sung here or a psalm appropriate to the day in Holy Week may be chanted in which case all stand.

The Gospel [All stand here if no Hymn or chant has preceded this reading]

The Missal is moved to the Gospel side of the Altar and the priest stands before the center of the Altar and prays, or blesses the Deacon.

Celebrant   May the Lord be in my heart and on my lips to announce the holy Gospel of peace.

The Priest goes to the Gospel side of the Altar to read the Gospel.

Gospeller   The Lord be with you.
People: *And also with you.*
Gospeller   The Holy Gospel of our Lord Jesus Christ according to _____.
People Glory to you, Lord Christ.

After the Gospel is finished, the Deacon blesses himself and kisses the book, saying

By this Gospel may our sins be wiped away.

The Sermon

The Offertory

Celebrant   The Lord be with you.
People And also with you.
Celebrant   Let us pray.

The Priest goes to the Gospel side and recites the Offertory Anthem. The Priest returns to the center and uncovers the chalice, and with hands on the Altar, says these or other prayers of preparation.

Celebrant   What shall I repay the Lord for all he has done for me? [*Taking the Chalice he says*] I will take the Chalice of salvation and will call upon the name of the Lord. [*Lifting the Chalice and Paten, he continues*] Receive, O Holy Trinity, this offering which I present to you in memory of the passion of our Lord Jesus Christ; and grant that it may ascend to you, pleasing in your sight, and may procure for me and all the faithful, eternal salvation.

The Little Liturgy of the Incense may be performed here.

The Celebrant then goes to the Epistle side and washes his fingers and prays silently

I will wash my hands among the innocent: and will encompass your Altar, O Lord, that I may hear the voice of praise, and tell of all your marvelous works. I have loved, O Lord, the beauty of your house, and the place where your glory dwells.

Returning to the center he bows solemnly and says

In humble spirit and with a contrite heart, may we be received by you, O Lord, and may our sacrifice be so performed, that it may be received by you today and may be pleasing to you, O Lord God.

The Celebrant turns to the People and invites them to join their prayers to his.

Celebrant Brothers and sisters, pray that my sacrifice and yours may alike be acceptable in the sight of the Lord.

Turning to the Altar he says

Lord, hear my prayer and let my cry come to you.

The Biddings

The Celebrant or Intercessor calls the People to prayers with these words.

I bid your prayers for the Holy Churches of God
throughout all the world.
I bid your prayers for [N. and N.] our bishop(s).
I bid your prayers for all Celebrants and deacons.
I bid your prayers for all members of God's Church.
I bid your prayers for the peace of the world.
I bid your prayers for those who suffer in body.
I bid your prayers for those who suffer in spirit.
I bid your prayers for those who seek God.
I bid your prayers for the departed. +
I bid your thanksgivings for the blessings
bestowed by our Lord.
I bid your praises for the ever-Blessed Virgin Mary, St.
Joseph, Blessed Dominic [Blessed N.] and all the Saints
who have gone before.

The Celebrant adds a concluding prayer, the Secret of the Mass.

People: *Amen.*

The Preface to the Canon

Celebrant   The Lord be with you.
People And also with you.
Celebrant   Lift up your hearts.
People We lift them to the Lord.
Celebrant Let us give thanks to the Lord our God.
People It is right to give him thanks and praise.

This Common Preface is said or sung when another is not appointed.

Celebrant   It is truly worthy and just, right and salutary, that we should always and in all places give you thanks, O Holy Lord, Father Almighty, Eternal God. Through Christ our Lord. Through whom the angels praise your majesty, the dominions adore, and the powers are in awe; the heavens and virtues of heaven and the blessed seraphim celebrate with united joy. With these we pray, may you join our voices also, while we say with lowly praise

Celebrant and People

Holy, holy, holy, Lord God of Hosts;
Heaven and earth are full of your glory.
Hosanna in the highest.
Blessed is he that comes in the name of the Lord.
Hosanna in the highest.

The Canon of the Mass

Celebrant   We therefore humbly pray and beseech you, most merciful Father, through Jesus Christ, your Son, our Lord, that you would vouchsafe to accept and bless these gifts, these presents, these holy and unspotted sacrifices; which in the first place we offer you for your holy Catholic Church, deign to grant her peace, as also to protect, unite and govern her throughout the whole world, together with your servant(s) [*N.* and *N,* and] *N.* our own Bishop, as also all believers and worshipers of the Catholic and Apostolic faith.

Be mindful, O Lord, [of your servants and handmaids [N and N], and] of all here present whose faith and devotion are known to you; for whom we offer, or who offer up to you this sacrifice of praise for themselves, their families and friends, for the redemption of their souls, for the hope of their safety and salvation, and who pay their vows to you the eternal, living and true God.

In communion with and veneration in the first place the memory of the glorious Ever- blessed Virgin Mary, the Mother of our Lord, Jesus Christ; and blessed Joseph, spouse of the same Virgin; blessed Dominic [N. whom we commemorate today] also of the blessed Apostles and Martyrs; and of all your saints; by whose prayers grant that we may always be defended by the help of your protection, through the same Christ our Lord. *Amen.*

We therefore beseech you, O Lord, graciously to accept this oblation of our service, and that of your whole family; dispose our days in your peace, grant us to be delivered from eternal damnation, and to be numbered in the flock of your elect, through Christ our Lord. *Amen.*

The Celebrant makes the sign of the Cross over the offerings, and once separately over the host and chalice.

Which oblation we beseech you, O God, deign to make blessed, approved, enrolled, ratified, reasonable and acceptable, that it may become for us the Body and Blood of your most beloved Son, our Lord Jesus Christ.

Who the day before he suffered, took bread into his holy and venerable hands, with his eyes lifted heavenwards to you, God, his almighty Father, giving you thanks, did bless, break and give to his disciples, saying, "Take and eat of this, all of you: for this is my Body."

In a like manner, after he had supped, taking this precious chalice into his holy and venerable hands, again giving You thanks, he blessed and gave it to his disciples saying, "Take and drink of this all of you: For this is the chalice of my Blood of the new and eternal testament, the mystery of faith which shall be shed for you, and for many, unto the remission of sins."

As often as you do these things, you shall do them in remembrance of me.

Wherefore, O Lord, we your servants, as also your holy people, calling to mind the blessed passion of the same Christ Your Son, our Lord, and also his resurrection from the grave, and glorious ascension into heaven, offer unto your most excellent majesty, of your gifts and grants.

The Celebrant makes the sign of the cross five times over the Body and Blood.

A pure victim, a holy victim, an immaculate victim, the holy Bread of eternal life, and the Chalice of everlasting salvation.

Upon which vouchsafe to look with a propitious and serene countenance, and to accept them, as you graciously were pleased to accept the gifts of your righteous servant Abel, and the sacrifice of our Patriarch Abraham, and that which your high Celebrant Melchisedech offered to you, a holy sacrifice, an immaculate host.

He bows profoundly and rising, kisses the Altar

We most humbly beseech you almighty God, command these things to be carried by the hands of your holy angel to your Altar on high, in the sight of your divine majesty; that as many of us, as by participation at this Altar, in the holy Body and Blood of your Son, may be filled with every heavenly blessing and grace through the same Christ our Lord. *Amen.*

Be mindful also, O lord, of your servants and handmaids who have gone before us with the sign of faith, and sleep in the slumber of peace, N. and N. To these, O Lord, and to all who rest in Christ, grant we beseech you, a place of refreshment, light, and peace through the same Christ our Lord. *Amen.*

And to us sinners, your servants, hoping in the multitude of your mercies, vouchsafe to grant some part and fellowship with your holy apostles and martyrs and with all your saints: into whose company we beseech you to admit us, not considering our merit, but freely pardoning our offenses through Christ our Lord. By whom, O Lord, you do always create, sanctify, endow with life, bless, and give us all these good things.

The Celebrant uncovers the chalice and genuflects. Rising, he makes the sign of the Cross with the sacred host five times saying

Through him, and with him, and in him; yours, God the Father Almighty, in the unity of the Holy Spirit, is all honor and glory for ever and ever. *AMEN!*

The Celebrant bows his head to the Body and Blood, then genuflects. Upon rising, he begins the Our Father in an audible voice.

Let us pray. Instructed by the saving precepts and following the divine directions, we presume to say

Celebrant and People

Our Father, who art in heaven, Hallowed be thy name. Thy kingdom come. Thy will be done on earth as it is in heaven. Give us this day our daily bread And forgive us our trespasses As we forgive those who trespass against us. And lead us not into temptation but deliver us from evil. For thine is the kingdom and the power and the glory for ever and ever. Amen.

Joining his hands the Celebrant prays

Deliver us, we beseech you, O Lord, from all evils, past, present, and to come; and by the intercession of the blessed and glorious Mary, ever a virgin, mother of God, together with thy blessed apostles Peter and Paul and Andrew, and all the saints, graciously grant peace in our days: what by the help of your mercy we may be always free from sin, and secure from disturbance. Through the same Jesus Christ, your Son, our Lord, who with you in the unity of the Holy Spirit, lives and reigns, God [*here he divides the Host*] world without end. *Amen.*

Celebrant: May the Peace of the Lord be always with you.
People: And also with you.

O Lamb of God, who takes away the sins of the world, have mercy upon us.
O Lamb of God, who takes away the sins of the world, have mercy upon us.
O Lamb of God, who takes away the sins of the world, grant us your peace.

The Celebrant then prays quietly.

May this most sacred commingling of the Body and Blood of our Lord Jesus Christ be to me and all who receive it, health of mind and body; and a saving preparation, winning and taking hold of life eternal. Through the same Christ our Lord. Amen.

O Lord Jesus Christ, Son of the Living God, who, according to the will of the Father, through the cooperation of the Holy Spirit, has by your death given life to the world; deliver me by this, your most sacred Body and Blood, from all my iniquities and from all evils; and make me ever cling to your commandments, and never suffer me to be separated from you; who with the same God, Father and the Holy Spirit lives and reigns God, for ever and ever. Amen.

Celebrant and People

Almighty and most merciful Father, we have erred and strayed from your ways like lost sheep, we have followed too much the devices and desires of our own hearts, we have offended against your holy laws, we have left undone the things which we ought to have done, and we have done the things which we ought not to have done. O Lord, have mercy upon us, spare those who confess their faults, restore those who are penitent, according to your promises declared unto mankind in Jesus Christ our Lord; and grant, O most merciful Father, for his sake, that we may ever hereafter live a godly, righteous and sober life, to the glory of your holy name. Amen.

Celebrant: May almighty God have mercy on you, and forgive you all of your sins; may he free you from all evil, save and strengthen you in every good work, and bring you to life everlasting. *Amen.*

or

Celebrant: May the Almighty and Merciful Lord grant you +absolution and remission of all your sins. *Amen.*

Celebrant: Behold the Lamb of God; behold Him who takes away the sins of the world.

Celebrant and People: Lord, I am not worthy that you should enter under my roof; but only say the word and my soul shall be healed.

The Celebrant receives into his mouth the Blessed Sacrament, saying

May the Body and Blood of our Lord Jesus Christ keep me unto life eternal. Amen.

[NOTE: In the Dominican Rite, the recipient does not generally respond with "Amen" as Communion is received.]

After the ablutions, the Celebrant then recites aloud.

May we receive into a pure heart, O Lord, what we have taken into our mouths, so that of the Body and Blood of our Lord Jesus Christ there may be made for us an everlasting healing. Amen.

The Celebrant purifies the Chalice and covers it he goes to the Epistle side of the altar, where the server has placed the book, to read the Communion Prayer.

Celebrant   The Lord be with you.
People   *And also with you.*
Celebrant   Almighty and everliving God we thank you for feeding us who have duly received these holy mysteries, with the spiritual food of the body and blood of your Son our savior Jesus Christ; and that you thereby assure us of your favor and goodness toward us and that we are members of the mystical body of your Son, which is the blessed company of all faithful people, and are heirs through hope of your everlasting kingdom by the merits of the most precious passion and death of your dear Son.

We humbly ask that you so assist us by grace that we may continue in that holy fellowship and all good works as you have prepared for us to walk in, through Jesus Christ our Lord, to whom with Father and Holy Spirit be all honor and glory throughout the ages of ages. *Amen.*

He then proceeds to the center of the altar and faces the people

Celebrant   The Lord be with you.
People   And also with you.
Celebrant   Let us pray
Celebrant and People: Almighty God we thank you for feeding us with the body and blood of your Son Jesus Christ our Lord. Through him we offer you ours souls and bodies to be a living sacrifice. Send us out in the power of Holy Spirit to live and work to your praise and glory. *Amen.*

Celebrant   The Lord be with you.
People And also with you.
Celebrant   Go, it has been offered.
People   Thanks be to God.

Celebrant [bowing] May the performance of my homage be pleasing to You, O Holy Trinity: and grant that the sacrifice which I, though unworthy, have offered in the sight of Your majesty, may be acceptable to You, and, through your mercy, may be a propitiation for me and for all those for whom I have offered it. Through Christ our Lord. Amen.

He kisses the altar, turns, and blesses the People, saying

May the blessing of Almighty God, Father, Son and Holy Spirit, descend upon you and remain with you forever. *Amen.*

The Altar Lights are extinguished. The People may remain in the Church for their own devotions.

Made in the USA
Charleston, SC
15 March 2012